GIFT OF A LIFETIME

A Woman's Guide to Triumphant Aging

GIFT
OF A
LIFETIME

A Woman's Guide
To Triumphant Aging

BARBARA STANFORD

LODGE HILL PRESS
Post Office Box 849 · Cambria, California 93428

Published by
Lodge Hill Press
Post Office Box 849
Cambria, CA 93428

Cover by Aldridge Design
Book design by Priscilla Trager
Printed and bound by
McNaughton & Gunn, Inc., Saline, Michigan

Several of these essays appeared in their original
form in *mergingTIMES*, a monthly newspaper
published in Paso Robles, California.
Grateful thanks to Flicka Dukes, publisher, for
supporting their republication.

ISBN 0-9652853-0-8

ACKNOWLEDGMENTS

When is a book conceived? Not, I believe, when the first words are written. Is it too much for me to go back, way back, to when I was a little girl, to the Depression years, to my father turning out novels as fast as he could write them to feed my mother, my sister and myself? He wrote whatever would sell: mystery, horror, romance, humor, even (as he sat in the London night writing in pencil on his yellow pad), yes, even westerns.

In the daytime, when I came home from school, I would read aloud from the yellow pad while he typed the manuscript on the heavy old typewriter: "Quote, capital letter, why, question mark, close quote, she said, full stop, new paragraph, capital letter..." on and on and on we went.

When the manuscript was typed (top copy and carbon) he bound the pages together using a little machine he had invented; a matter of making holes in the pages then tying the book together with string. A piece of brown wrapping paper made the cover, the title and his name carefully written on the front with pen dipped in ink. Work completed, his socks must be darned; the frayed collar of his shirt unstitched, "turned", and stitched back on again to look, perhaps, like new; the sleeves of his musty overcoat hid the worn shirt cuffs. Then, off to his agent, Mr. Lewin in Central London. Without sufficient money for the fare he walked the first part of the journey then paid a penny for the bus that would take him the rest of the way ("Walk a penny, ride a penny," we used to call it.) Next night, the yellow pad, another book, another small check.

This was our life until the War changed everything: we children evacuated to Cornwall, my father in a Bristol aircraft factory, my mother keeping us all together as a family. My brother, born later, became a writer, and now I know that writing is in my blood, that I am part of a family of writers, that writing is what we do.

But not only the past has created this book. In the last few years so many people, knowingly and unknowingly, have played their part. I thank the members of my "Over Fifty" women's groups who told me more than they knew; the readers of my newspaper articles who supported me more than they knew; Flicka Dukes who got me started then stayed to encourage; Anne Phillips who took an interest from the start; Judy Appelbaum who taught me so much; Sally Thomson who asked to read the manuscript; Margaret Nemoede who spoke wise words; Marnie Burkhardt who told me a story; Mikhail Ann Long who lived her life; Peggy Gray who knew about "solo"; Eddie Palmer who was touched by the Buddha; John and Tish Allan who gave me good advice; Barbara Garn who came to the rescue; my children, Adam and Nina, who always support Mom; Lyn, my given child, who knows what I write about; and Douglas Pillsbury who teaches me how to be loving and patient and kind.

To My Readers

If you wish to order more copies of this book, send a check or money order for $9.95 (includes mailing) for each book to:

Lodge Hill Press
Post Office Box 849
Cambria, CA 93428

Once you have read this book you may find you have comments to make. Do you have concerns about a loved one who is aging? Do you have thoughts about your own aging? Write to me at the above address. I will be pleased to hear from you and you will hear from me.

For information about personal telephone consultations, workshops, and talks, direct inquiries to:

Dr. Barbara Stanford
at Lodge Hill Press.

GIFT OF A LIFETIME

A Woman's Guide to Triumphant Aging

Age: maturity, majority, seniority.

Aging: maturing, ripening, mellowing.

Gift: something given voluntarily without charge,
a favor, a blessing.

To triumph: to prevail, withstand, overcome, surpass,
rejoice, celebrate.

Triumphant: undefeated, crowned, victorious.

CONTENTS

Starting Out

Working Through

Being Alone

Planning Ahead

Moving On

Starting Out

Retirement...What's That?

When I told people I was retiring they grabbed my hand, pumped it up and down, smiled ear-to-ear, and said, "Congratulations! That's great!" I used to stand there, wondering, "What do they mean? What are they congratulating me for?"

I still don't understand. Were they recognizing the completion of a career? Twenty years on a college faculty is a long time that needs to be recognized; so I thank them if they were congratulating me on my years of work. Or were they congratulating me, not for ending something but for beginning my years of retirement, for starting out on that period of my life (10 years, 20, 25, dare I consider 30?) when, as someone wrote to me, "the years might be like a never-ending summer vacation"?

Ending and beginning. That's what all of life's transitions are: puberty, coming of age, graduations, the first day at work, marriage, parenthood. That's what retirement is: one period of life is over and now we move on to the new. And after so many years of living we do not move on unprepared. During the long years our ideas have been formed, our habits have been developed, our skills have been crafted, our knowledge has been accumulated, our affiliations have been forged. It is with these accomplishments that we face our future.

But there's a problem with retirement that's unlike any other turning point. We walk into our new life without a map. A map is a guide. It tells us where we are, where we can go and how to get there. It tells us what sort of road we'll be on: whether it's rough or smooth, hilly or flat, softly wooded or a desolate plain. It lets us see we have options in deciding where we will go and choices in how we want to get there.

Other turning points come with a map. When we were young we had a very clear idea of what to do with our years: to lay down the foundation of our lives as adults and to build upon that foundation. Those were the years of creating: creating a marriage, a home, a career, having babies and helping them grow into the adults they eventually became. We say our life was "mapped out."

Retirement isn't like that. No one tells us what is expected of us, how we should be, what we should do. In fact, the word "retirement" means "withdrawing". So we withdraw from work and career, we step off the stage into the wings, and then...what then? Silence.

So we have to do it ourselves and that's hard. A little guide-book, a few precious inches of map, would make retirement so much easier. Without that help it can feel lonely and frightening.

Some of the fear comes from the realization that retirement is inextricably tied to getting older. The truth that is never mentioned is that retirement is the gateway to old age. The longer we live, the further we move away from our working years, the more we are seen, not as retired, but as old, and then as very old. These are the unspoken facts and they bring disturbing questions. When will I stop being "retired" and start being "old"? How long do I have? Will I have enough money to live decently? Accustomed to making decisions about our lives we recognize that perhaps, one day, we may be less in control. What will that be like? What will happen to me? Will my health hold up? Who will I depend on? Yes, it is time to live an easier life but will it really be like a never-ending summer vacation?

So, while the retirement parties emphasize the hearty, jolly congratulations, while the well-wishers smile and joke, the person leaving the security of work and middle-age finds herself with mixed feelings. She says nothing for there is an agreement of silence. People do not want to know. Expressing concern is not welcome. It reminds the others of their future; that one day they will be asking the same questions, feeling the same feelings. And so the friends return to the reassurance of work and middle-age and the retired person sets out on her uncertain journey.

Given that we do not know, as we move toward old age, what the future will bring, we understand why we have no map. We cannot draw a map of unknown territory. Perhaps it helps to remember that all of our life has had its element of unknown territory, less unknown when we were younger perhaps, but still not absolutely certain. The five-year plan usually doesn't work out even when we are in our twenties but we write it anyway. It sets us on a path, it gives us a direction with goals and hopes, it gives meaning to life, it prevents the unpleasant feeling of drifting, of purposelessness.

Victor Frankl, the psychologist survivor of the concentration camps, tells us that those who survived were those able to find meaning in their life no matter how little meaning seemed possible. The person who stayed alive for a loved one, the person who had a great work to accomplish when the nightmare ended, the person who believed that God had placed him there for a reason: these were the survivors. In the same way retirement and its entry into old age, even while the future cannot be known, can become a full and rewarding experience when it is seen as having meaning.

So often I have the impression that those who are retiring do not see their future years as having any special meaning. They have no idea of the gift they are being offered, of the potential that the later years hold. They seem just to drift into this period of their life. The important years have come to an end. There is not much more to be said or done. They hope that what's left will be enjoyable.

It seems a very passive approach when you consider the years of experience and accomplishment that every woman and man of sixty must have had. But perhaps the passivity is rooted not in ourselves but in our society. The old are seen as weak, sick, dependent and ugly. And we, when young, accepted, on some level, these cultural beliefs: they have become deeply a part of us. Now the day has come when it is not "them" that we disparage, but "us", and "me". It is not surprising that some people as they age should see their life in negative ways.

Old age is neither the jolly, hearty time of the retirement parties, nor is it the sad, lonely, sick time of our cultural messages. It may sometimes be a little of both but it is also more: much, much more. For our long past life has prepared us well. We remember that this is not the first time we have experienced a turning point in our lives. Graduation from college, marriage, the first child, the famous mid-life crisis: these were all turning points. We remember how we wondered and worried, we recall the fears we had, how confused and unprepared we felt as we faced these new experiences.

And it is here that we find our strength. For we lived through those times and moved on. We bumbled and fumbled, we did things wrong and put them right, we felt uncertain then we gained in confidence, we learned how to live through challenging times, difficult times, and times that were downright bad.

When we look back we realize that the years have, in fact, given us the sweet gifts of experience and wisdom. We know that we can live through uncertainty. We know that we have developed inner strength, resilience, and fortitude. We realize that the accumulated years are on our side: we have learned how to live.

And so it is with these gifts of experience and wisdom that we face yet another time of change and challenge. Our culture may have given us no map but our very age will tell us where we wish to go and how to get there.

Now, at last, as we enter old age, we have the opportunity to use what we have taken so long to learn. Now we can say, "At last I have the wisdom to know who I am. In the years I have left I can nurture and develop my important, matured self. Finally, I can fully realize the potential of what has always been within me. What rewards and meaning my old years are going to have!" Truly the gift of a lifetime!

THE SUNSET YEARS

Ours is not an introspective nation. Looking inward is not what Americans do. Instead we value work, activity, progress. Meaning in our life is associated with production, achievement, and the accumulation of money, property and things. Ours is a nation of getting ahead, climbing the career ladder, having more, "I'm on my way!"

These values are so deeply ingrained they are hard to change. But are they appropriate for the later years? Most older people no longer wish to be so active and striving. We don't need more things or more property. Though some would like more money there often seems to be no way of getting it. Opportunities for paid work are frequently closed to older people.

The psychologist, Carl Jung, called youth "life's morning" and age, "life's afternoon". He wrote: " ...for what was great in the morning will be little in the afternoon...for the aging person it is a necessity to give serious attention to *himself*. After having lavished its light upon the world, the sun withdraws its rays in order to illume itself." So the task of aging, he is saying, is not to succeed out there in the world, but to turn inward and "illume" oneself.

But what can we find if we turn inward? Isn't it the young who have knowledge and creativity and inspiration? Aren't the old "past their prime", "over the hill"? What can possibly be hidden within that is worth looking for?

Jung's mention of the sun reminds us of its great trajectory across the sky. There is the quiet beginning, the rise in force and passion, the fall and the setting before it is lost to our view. Old age is that setting, "the sunset years" as the advertisements tell us, and if the sun were simply to slip quietly away then old age might be seen as a time of being "over the hill": but that is not what happens. In fact, the sun's setting is the most astonishing part of its journey.

The daytime sun is a yellow disc, hard, and dangerous to look at. In the evening we experience the miracle. Now softened, we can watch without fear as the setting sun fills the sky, its color and form always different, a glorious, triumphant, astonishing display. We do nothing to deserve its munificence. It is a gift just given, just handed to us. Is it possible that our later years are life's astonishing gift?

On some evenings the setting sun is hidden by clouds but the sun is still setting. We would see its glory if the clouds were not there so when we deny the gift of age are we not creating the clouds that hide the setting sun? If we compare age to youth and find age inferior, if we wish for the past again, if we try to act and look "young", if we fear getting older, if we believe that old age means Alzheimer's disease and nursing homes, then it is impossible to accept our later years as a valued gift. We are creating the destructive attitudes that hide the importance of age.

In a society like our own, where youth is so valued, it is understandable that we should fear old age and see it only as a time of sad decline. Even when we know that the years ahead need not be a sad experience it is hard to change the attitudes of a lifetime. But if we can find a way to accept age as it is, with its own integrity, possibilities, and rewards, then we are free to give "serious attention", as Jung says, to ourselves as an older person. Then we can ask, "How can I make the most of this astonishing gift of age? How can I illume myself?"

Each person will answer these questions differently for each of us has lived a different life, but it is the asking of the questions that is important. For in saying, "How can I use this astonishing gift of age?" we free ourselves from the fears of sad deterioration. Instead, we welcome the opportunity to live the "sunset years" in our own, important, and very personal way.

A THOUSAND MOMENTS

The time went by so fast," she said, "the time went by so fast." Holding my hand, pain and fear in her voice, in her huge eyes, in her thin, old body; seeing everything suddenly collapsing, he close to death, she just diagnosed with a serious illness.

Where did it go, the time, where did it go? In making the soup and driving the car and helping the children with their homework and sewing on buttons and staying late at the office and watching television and hammering nails and going to the movies and taking out the garbage and staying in motels and decorating the Christmas tree and reading the newspaper and washing our hands. And now it is coming to an end.

Is my life coming to its end, I wonder? Perhaps I will be killed on the highway tomorrow. Have I told my love how much I love him, have I told him enough, have I really experienced the moments with him? Have I felt closeness with my children? Do I know what it means to be with my own flesh, my own blood? Do I experience the awful magic intensity of life? Or am I still making the soup, driving the car, sewing on buttons? At sixty-seven how long do I have? One day or thirty years? Will it end fast? Or will I go slowly, lingeringly, declining, fading away?

I do not know. We do not know. We have the time we have. That must be enough.

How hard it is to "grab" the life one has lived: a jumble of events, a journey of places, a haze of sensations, a bubbling of feelings. It all brings us here, to this place, this body, these memories, these abilities, these people, this moment. This is what we have. This is what will accompany us as we start our journey of one day or thirty years.

When I look back over my life I see it as a painting with large brush strokes: England, the Second World War, Italy, marriage, America, children, UCLA, teaching, retiring. There are small brush-strokes as well: the smell of chrysanthemums on a cold day in England, collecting drinking water from the fountain in Rome, the Statue of Liberty early one December morning as our ship approached the New World, the New Life.

And what do I want for the one day to thirty years that I have left? I know I am less interested than I used to be in the big brush-strokes. Striving, I can see, is for the young, for the middle-aged. Now I am ready to settle down with my writing, my counseling, a little bit of teaching. I have built the house of my life and now I just want to live in it. I want my life to be small.

For I realize at last that small is what life is all about. Life, fully lived, is not years or months or days or even hours. Life is moments, tiny moments that are so hard to notice. We don't pay attention. We go too fast.

We catch a fleeting glance, hear the tone of a voice, glimpse the new moon, and let the moment go. We are so busy trying to get our point across, listening to the news, having another cup of coffee, that we have no time to notice the moments of our lives. And we do it with our partners as well. We can live for ten, twenty, forty years together, amicably, busily, pleasantly, the fight now and then, but hardly ever really saying, really noticing, really paying attention to the other. How often we hear people say with regret, "I didn't have time to tell her how much I loved her." How often we hear of people saying that it was only when they had a serious illness that they were able to live their life. "Cancer has been a gift," they say.

Isn't it strange? It is when we are reminded that our life is limited that we start to live it. Only then do we pay attention to our own existence.

So let us observe the moments, the moments as they pass. Let us be thankful for each one of them, and let us be thankful for those who share our life of moments. Let us tell them how good they are, how grateful we are, how much we love them.

And then a miracle happens.

Away goes unhappiness for unhappiness is killed by gratitude. When we pay attention to the moments we find that we can choose the way we feel. We don't have to be upset or angry about most things that happen to us. We can make a tiny shift and see the situation as it is: just there, neither right nor wrong, neither good nor bad. We can just be with it, just go along with it. And when we do that the moment is always right and good.

Away, too, go old resentments. We can learn to tell a new story of our life, not the sad, angry old story we have told ourselves and others for years. I rewrote my story. I pulled out the good things, the blessings my mother, my father, my life had given me. I found many. In fact, the more I thought the more I found and I'm still remembering more blessings. I threw away the things that had angered me for years. With all those blessings, why burden myself with that sad, boring bag of self-righteous stories? I haven't missed them a bit. As the bumper sticker says, "It's Never Too Late to Have Had a Happy Childhood".

When we discard the upset we feel clear, accepting, grounded, no longer blown about by the winds of change. We become grateful for what we have had and ready for what is to come no matter what it may be. Now life is no longer one day to thirty years, it is thousands and thousands and thousands of moments.

MISS WHITE AND MISS BROWN

I remember Miss White and Miss Brown. In London, before the Second World War changed all our lives, they lived in the flat upstairs. Two maiden ladies as they were called; sisters, I presume. Miss White had her own white hair, soft and wavy. Her face was pretty, her body pleasingly plump. Miss Brown was thin, her face haggard and gray. She wore a drab, hopeless wig, straight brown hair pulled back into an inadequate bun. They were very quiet, very slow, very wrinkled, very old.

Perhaps they had experienced more affluent times or maybe I think this because I saw them only on the stairs, going up and down from their flat. The ragged carpet could not hide the beauty of those wide and generous stairs, their perfect, sweeping curve a reminder of a more expansive, Victorian age. I remember the two old sisters stepping with great dignity, backs straight, heads high.

I have no idea who they were, what lives they had lived. For me, a little girl, they were simply old, impossibly old. They were frighteningly different from everything I knew about being human. They walked the stairs, they smiled, they spoke to me, the little girl who lived downstairs. And because they were so strange I was afraid. When they appeared I did not know what to do. Should

I stay as they passed or could I run away? I was fascinated, which pulled me to stay. But I did not want to be close to them which urged me to run.

When they spoke their quiet words I could think of no reply. I stood, my back to the wall, pulling down my skirt, watching as they slowly turned to mount the stairs, then darting off, released, free, young, light, no longer in danger, absolved, reprieved.

I realize now how poor they must have been (as we were), how lonely their lives, how each must have feared the other dying first. But we never knew them. They were separate, alien creatures because they were old.

And now that little girl is old though not as old, perhaps, as they were. My hair has not turned white nor do I wear a brown wig but I am old to those who are little girls today. Are they afraid of me? Maybe they sometimes are. The things they have said to me, "You're old," "Why do you have so many wrinkles?" separates me from them, perhaps. For those little girls I am a strange creature.

Even when others are not very young, maybe even adult, I have to remember that I am seen as "old" and therefore different, though I know that I am not all that different. My young girl, my young adult, lives right here with me. I am just more complex, more richly layered. I am more thoughtful, more intelligent, more patient, more compassionate. There is more to me than there used to be.

Now that I am old I understand, I really understand, what "Black is Beautiful" is all about. It is about pride; it is about the richness of being who you are. I understand, too, the power of that little slogan, for words create ideas and ideas can change the world. What must it be like, I wonder, to grow up in a society where "Old is Beautiful"? Because it's the growing-up time that does the damage. We're so unthinking then. We don't know what's happening to us. We accept it all. What a different experience it would be if the young grew up knowing "Old is Beautiful".

All I can do now is to love Miss White and Miss Brown, say I'm sorry, admire their quiet dignity. All I can do now is be old in my own way, as they were.

Planning Your Old Life and Making It Good

An Exercise in Triumphant Aging

Perhaps the key to a good old age lies with your feelings and assumptions about yourself as an old person. If you hate the idea of being old then efforts at creating a good old life will be defeated by a mind that is saying "No" to existing at all. You cannot hate your aging and, at the same time, plan a good old life. It is only when you value your aging that you can create your own special good old life.

Here are two paper-and-pencil exercises that may help you clarify the reality of your present aging experience.

Take a pen and some paper. Down the left-hand side of the paper, numbered 1 through 6, write: I am sick, I am forgetful, I am lonely, I am asexual, I am poor, I am senile. Across the top of the paper write the headings for 5 columns: All the time, A lot, Sometimes, Rarely, Never. Prepare this table on three pieces of paper. Now, sit down somewhere quiet with enough time to allow yourself to ponder the questions I am asking you.

Exercise 1.

The six statements you have written are our cultural stereotypes of aging. This is what we have learned about being old.

Using one of your prepared tables, fill in the responses that describe you *at the present time*.

Examine what you have stated about yourself. Do you want to change anything you have written?

Now do the exercise again describing *the way you were twenty years ago*.

Is there a great deal of difference between you today and you twenty years ago? If you had looked into the future then, would you have expected to describe yourself as you do now?

Now do the exercise again. *In twenty years I will be:*

You have now completed your personal picture of those aspects of living into old age that concern many people. What picture have you drawn? If you have described a future of decline what is the basis for your assumptions? Are you describing your true reality or are you allowing the cultural stereotypes to tell you how you are and how you will be? Remember that to a large degree we can decide how our life will be. So, with you in control, do you wish to change any aspect of the next twenty years? Allow yourself, during the next days, to make some decisions about how you want to be as you get older.

Exercise 2.

In this exercise you can start to appreciate the many ways in which your life is getting, not worse, but better.

Write down all the ways in which you are wiser, happier, more adaptable, stronger, etc. than you were when you were young. It is very helpful to think of an example (or examples) of each improvement and write that down as well. This means, for example, that instead of a vague, non-specific claim to greater adaptability, you support the claim with a specific example of something that happened, say, last week. You then "know" this about yourself in a demonstrably concrete way. Thus:

1. I am more patient. An example is...
2. I am more appreciative of nature's wonders. An example is...
3. I am wiser than I used to be. An example is...

Continue in this way. Over the next days keep thinking about it. Don't be shy. Enjoy documenting the improvements in you and in your life. Notice how you have changed for the better and write these things down. I think you will see that your life has deepened. You will realize how much you carry into your future that is positive.

It is important for us to pay attention to the gifts that a lifetime has given us because it is only when we recognize them and embrace them that we can use them to help make our old life a good life. There is a difference between *being* more patient and *knowing* you are more patient. Consciousness of who you are allows you to respond to situations in a more highly developed way. Knowing your new strength allows you to greet life with a self-assurance that was not possible when you were younger. Yes, it is strange, given the negative cultural stereotypes about the old, to believe that you can experience yourself with greater self-assurance, but that is what will happen if you embrace the knowledge that you now have about yourself as an old woman.

In order to look forward to an old life that is good we have to put aside the old, worn cultural stereotypes.

We also have to stop comparing ourselves with the young. The characteristics of the young are perfect for the young but unsuitable for the old. Instead, let us give thanks for all the new and special gifts we are given as we get older. It is these gifts that we need as we move confidently and gratefully into the future.

Working Through

The Daily Round; the Common Task

It seems so unfair. He goes off to work, smelling like a rose. You are left with the dirty dishes. Even when you both work outside the home you are still left with the dirty dishes. He "helps". Eventually you both retire. He no longer goes to work. You no longer go out to work but your other work, housework, never ends. Women who work outside the home have two jobs. When they "retire" they have one. In this sense, women never retire. The dirty dishes never go away.

So, now that neither of you goes out to work how are you going to get the housework done? If a man sees it as "woman's work" he may be unwilling to do it. He would feel awkward, out-of-place, even demeaned if he cleaned the toilet. His responsibilities will be the garden, the car, minor repairs, financial matters. You will continue to cook and clean, do the laundry and the shopping: the more time-consuming part. Some women prefer it that way. The old arrangement feels right to them. They enjoy it.

Others resent it. The daily demands of running a household use up a woman's time. Every day there are many small (and large) tasks to attend to, tasks that eat into the hours women would prefer to spend in some other way. While a woman may accept this as her responsibility before retirement she is often unwilling to do so after retirement. At last she wants to have equal time with her husband. Finally, she hopes, the daily round of housework can be shared so that she has uninterrupted time to do other things.

Sometimes a husband (and I hear this complaint often) attempts to take over the household tasks. Fresh out of forty years in management it's clear that his wife doesn't know how to run the house. He barges into the kitchen and reorganizes everything according to the efficiency principles learned at work. Then he is shocked when his wife says, "Get out of my kitchen!"

Even when a husband attempts to do his share with more sensitivity, it can be difficult for his wife to accept his efforts. We all experience feelings of self-worth from the things we have done for many years and learned to do well. Running a household, doing it skillfully, gives a woman control and power. When a husband wants to do his share, a woman may see herself losing that control, power, and self-worth.

So it is possible for a woman to resent it if her husband does not share the housework and resent it if he does! A husband may feel uncomfortable if he doesn't do his share of the housework and uncomfortable if he does!

Whether a marriage is a long one or more recent, patterns of behaving and relating have been quickly formed. A couple is often unaware of the way they relate to each other. As the years have passed the two behaviors (what he does, what she does) have meshed, easily or not. Life together has become routine. There seems to be no other way. Even the imperfections, the accustomed irritations, are reassuring. The familiarity of married life gives comfort for it is predictable in this world where so little is predictable.

Retirement brings change to this familiar life together. The big change is obvious: he, or she, or he and she, no longer go out to work each day. The big adaptation is obvious, too: how to live on a reduced income and what to do with the extra time. While figuring out how to deal with these major changes, it would be so reassuring if the small details of life together could continue as before. Too much change is disconcerting. If feels as if there is nothing to depend on any more.

But our personal lives, like our society, our world, our very universe, are systems of inter-related parts. Change one thing and everything else changes. If we ignore this we get ourselves into trouble for the inevitable results of change will not go away. It is we that will suffer as we remain always out of step. The change that retirement brings creates a shift in all the details of married life. There are many adaptations to make, and one of these adaptations is fitting the housework into this new, changed life.

If ever there is a time when a couple needs to be flexible it is when they retire. If ever there is a time when husband and wife need to communicate, honestly but kindly, it is now. The early months of retirement are truly a setting down of a new, long period of life. It is as important to get things right now as it was when a couple first married. Then, all those years ago, difficulties may have existed because of youth and inexperience. It took some time, perhaps, to work it all out. Now difficulties exist because the way things have been done for all these years is so familiar. There is a reluctance to examine and change an arrangement that has worked well enough for so long.

But life together is no longer the way it used to be. At some time, and sooner is better than later, a retired couple has to accept that many changes have occurred and that they need to respond to them all. Housework, because of its daily occurrence, is a good place to start. If a wife can tell her husband about her mixed feelings, that she wants him to share the household duties but feels diminished when he does, then maybe he can move very gently into her territory. If a husband can tell his wife that he wants to share the work but feels awkward when he does, then she can respect the tension he experiences. In a marriage there are two people going through this process of change so this means a double task: dealing with one's own response to the change and patiently supporting one's partner's efforts at adapting as well. This is not easy to do. We can feel anxious, critical, angry, awkward, as we go through this new process. We may wonder whether it's worth bothering about.

But the details of our lives, even the most mundane, are worth bothering about. Their very ordinariness means that they happen daily and therefore affect our lives powerfully. If we get it right then we are free to enjoy retirement without constant, daily irritation. And in getting it right, in working out the details, in being patient and forgiving, the marriage bond is strengthened as the couple faces the remainder of their life together.

CHILD OF MY CHILD

I plan to spend more time with my grandchildren," people say when thinking about retirement. And what a delightful experience they look forward to! Free from the responsibilities of parenting, relating to grandchildren in new ways, the relationship can be care-free and irresistible. There is also the opportunity to do things better than we did with our own children. The trouble with parenting is that we have no practice before we plunge into it! When the grandchildren come along we have had time to think about what we did and make fewer mistakes the second time around.

The grandmother role becomes whatever we wish to make of it. Some grandmothers just want to have fun. They want the relationship with their grandchildren to be light and happy: going places, buying treats, reading books together, having good experiences that both remember with pleasure. Some become the teacher as they read together, search the tide-pools, knit a scarf.

Other grandmothers take the opportunity to share the special richness of their long lives with their grandchildren. I think of the person who can listen, thoughtfully, with patience, without criticism. I think of the old who can introduce to the young a different way of looking at life. No longer so goal-directed, so striving,

31

so impatient for results, she can gently show her grandchild what she has learned: to see the whole picture, to know that time passes, that everything is necessary and everything fits in. People call this wisdom: a gift that comes to us when we have lived a long life and thought about it as well. Planting the seeds of wisdom is, for the child, the beginning of wisdom.

Grandparents can also be a help to a troubled child. In my work as a counselor I have noticed how often my clients, in talking to me about their childhood, say, "I used to go to my grandmother's house. She knew what was going on. She would hold me, let me stay with her. She was the only person I felt safe with."

Grandmothering gives warmth, safety and understanding in a young life that is troubled and hurt. My clients have different memories of what they found in their grandmother's house. Some found a chance to pour out their story of trouble. Some found a quiet, ordered haven offering peace and relief from the shouting and chaos at home. Some went for the doing and learning they could find nowhere else: cooking, sewing, painting, gardening. Years later these understanding grandmothers are remembered with tremendous affection and honored with deep thanks.

One grandmother I know has such a relation with a granddaughter who lives far away. They don't allow the physical distance to interfere with their important relationship. The girl knows she can call grandma when her unhappy home life becomes unbearable. They have long talks on the telephone and it helps: the child knows that she is not alone, the grandmother knows that she is helping a child get through difficult years. In a troubled life if there is one person who listens, who understands, who is always there, then somehow the child may survive. A grandparent is often that person. They don't get mixed up in the battle, they don't interfere in what is going on at home, they stay outside the fray, they listen and care, and that is enough. There are many ways to be a grandmother.

But, even so, when people say, "I plan to spend more time with my grandchildren," I always want to respond, "And do your grandchildren plan to spend more time with you?" That would sound harsh so I may not say it but somehow the question needs to be asked – and answered.

Years ago, in rural America, the family was a working unit. Each member had tasks appropriate to sex and age and relationships developed through shared work and everyday experiences. Today life is no longer such a family affair. The children grow up and leave home; grandchildren are born in other cities, other states, other countries; shared work and everyday experiences are replaced with weekend visits, holiday get-togethers, cards and gifts sent through the mail. There is frequently a desire for closer ties but the grown children are busy with their jobs, their homes, and raising their children.

When the grandchildren are very young and live nearby, grandmothers may fit easily into their lives. The world of a young child is small: parents, siblings, the home, toys, books. There is a lot of room for a grandmother who plays with them, cuddles them, takes them out. But as children become involved in school, move into adolescence, make their own friends, find their own interests, there is less and less time left for family. Their peer group becomes important with its strange sound they call music, trendy clothes, cosmetics, fads, sports, television, school work, sex, and money. (High school students spend an average of $3,000 a year!). Grandmothers can feel more and more left out.

If grandchildren live far away and are rarely seen it is hard to build a valuable relationship. Phone calls, cards and gifts keep the channels of communication open but there is not enough time spent together to create strong bonds. For those who feel the lack of the grandmother role there seems to be a void that can never be filled.

Perhaps it is then that a hard question needs to be asked: does the desire to spend more time with the family come from a wish for closer, loving ties, or from a need to fill up the extra time that retirement gives? Is the time with the family sought because it will nourish "them " as well as "me", or is the real purpose nourishing "me"? Is this the new, deepening relationship that everyone has been waiting for, or is it a way to combat loneliness and the emptiness of too much unstructured time? These are hard questions to ask and sometimes harder to answer honestly, for there is a fine line between maintaining family bonds and using the family to compensate for having little life of one's own.

Relying on others to fill up one's time and to make sense of one's life when those others are unable or unwilling to do so must result in a lonely, rejected, hopeless feeling. Ideally, this sad experience will compel a woman to face her own lack of interests and resources. It may lead her to realize that no matter how old she may be, each of us has the responsibility to create our own meaningful life. We must not expect others to do this for us.

This is a hard and unexpected lesson to learn for we were not prepared for the changes in family relations that have happened during this century. When we were children the family was more likely to be close by;

the adolescent, peer-group culture was less dominant; the young did not expect to have so many possessions, so much money; there were not so many distractions to pull them away from family.

Life is strange. As E. M. Forster wrote in *A Room with a View:* "Life is a public performance on the violin, in which you must learn the instrument as you go along." We want to give a fine performance, to appear to be doing well in the eyes of others. We want, also, to be doing well in our own eyes. After all, this is our life, our one life, this is all we've got. How can we live it well? How can we live our old age well? How can we be good grandmothers in this new world where people seem to have less time to share?

I remember a man, a middle-aged man, who had lost his whole family in the holocaust. He told me how much he had missed, and still missed, having had grandparents. I do not know why he felt this particular lack so deeply but he did. It occurred to me that there are many children who, because of geographical distance, divorce or death, lack a grandparent, and many grandparents who, for the same reasons, lack a grandchild.

Is it possible, I wondered, for a woman, lacking the opportunity to experience fully the grandmother role with her own grandchildren, to become a grandmother to a needy child? Does the child have to belong to one's own child? Does blood play an imperative part? In order to love the child is it essential that one looks at him and thinks, "This is the child of my child"? Without that is it impossible for the grandmother relationship to develop?

Some people are able to imagine themselves sharing a loving relationship with a child who is not the child of their child. And they will find that once the dream is dreamed the child comes along: mentioned by someone at church, read about in the local newspaper. Somewhere the child exists, waiting to be found.

We don't need money. We don't even need a biologically related child. To be a good grandparent we need only to be loving and kind to those who are still learning how to live.

Forgotten Dreams

The child dreams. Her small world is vast. Nothing is impossible, nothing foolish. She dreams of faraway places, of sacrificing her young life to service for others, of the wildly adoring Broadway crowd. "One day I'll do that."

We've all had a dream but somewhere, somehow, the dream got lost. Raising a family, money, illness, war, parents who imposed their own needs onto their children: all kinds of things prevented us from fulfilling our dream. It was put aside. Eventually it seemed to be forgotten.

I remember going to a physician for a series of visits. He didn't seem to enjoy being a physician and I soon realized that he wasn't a good one so I stopped going. I had the impression that he would rather have been a cowboy than a doctor. Later I heard that he had sold his practice and gone off, alone, in a camper. Perhaps I was right about the cowboy! Maybe, in being a physician he was fulfilling his parents' dream and it wasn't until he was in his middle age that he was able to say, "I'm grown up now and I'm not going to pretend to be a physician any more. I'm going to fulfill my own dream."

Like him we know that the dream may fade but it never goes away. It nudges at us, that small, deep regret,

"If only…if only I'd had the chance at least to try…well, it was just a silly dream…it's too late now." What are we thinking about when we say, "It's too late now"? The number we write on a form for our age? Our wrinkles and sagging body and graying hair? Are we noticing that older people don't do the kind of things we dream of doing? Does that mean that we may not do them, either?

It seems ridiculous that a woman called "Senior Citizen" would remember the dream of that child who, so many years ago, believed that everything was possible. But when we say," It was just a silly dream," we know, in that secret, private part of ourselves, that the dream was not silly. We dream our dreams for a reason. They do not just pop up out of nowhere. They have powerful significance for us. Denying our dreams leaves a hole that will never be filled.

I remember giving a workshop for married couples. There was an exercise to be done in which the husband and wife, separately, were to make a list of things they wanted to do in retirement. One purpose of the exercise was that each would state their desires without the influence of their partner. One wife refused to do it alone. She insisted on doing it with her husband. She said, "We always agree." I had noticed in the group that the husband spoke, she remained silent. I wondered how much of herself she had buried as, over the years, she became no more than her husband's shadow. Not an idea of her own, not a wish that was hers, not a whisper of independence and autonomy. I wondered what dreams she may have had, dreams that now would never be realized. Like the middle-aged physician who perhaps lived his parents' dreams, she continued to live her husband's.

Fulfilling our dreams helps us to grow towards completeness and surely one task of our older years is to find completeness. We need to find the value our life has had in the past and decide what value it can have in the future. We must remind ourselves that the expression of our very personal talents, interests, and longings is important. To decide that retirement and old age is the time to do those things which have been put aside for so long is to take one's life seriously, to know that it has value.

In a society that does not see the old as valuable it is difficult for us to cut across the cultural stereotypes, for we, too, have accepted the lies. Many of the old, in their attitude to their own old age, are like the wife who always agreed with her husband. They find it easier to go along with society's expectations and fade away, uncomplaining but unfulfilled. This only perpetuates the lie that the old have nothing of value to offer any more.

But some, by returning to their past, find the inspiration to make the later years important and interesting. Then, younger people, seeing that the old can value themselves and behave in interesting ways, find themselves valuing the old. It is by changing our behavior that we change ourselves, and it is by changing ourselves that we start to change the world. Perhaps our half-forgotten dreams can point the way.

These dreams that stay with us, hidden for so many years, quietly but insistently remind us, nudge us, let us know there is something we need to do; not because someone else wants us to do it or because we will get paid for it; not for any extrinsic reward, but simply because our being is crying out for us to do it, that it is good in and of itself, that we will experience ourselves on another, higher level. And when we do such things it is always right for ourselves and for the world.

During the hectic years of early marriage, work,

housework, raising a family, we got so accustomed to fulfilling the needs of others we no longer knew what our own, personal needs were. They became so buried within us that we were hardly aware of those things we wanted to do for ourselves. But when we are older and the demands of work and family are less urgent, then we can and should make a choice about how we wish to live the rest of our life.

Those who dare to look into their past will find that their hidden dreams, denied for so many years, are still there and still asking to be fulfilled. There, too, is that priceless belief that nothing is impossible, nothing is foolish. It may not be possible to realize the dream as a twenty-year-old might have done, but we can adapt it to our wiser age. No longer caught up by dreams of melodramatic sacrifice for others we can now consider the more prosaic Peace Corps. They have no upper age-limit for accepting applicants. Or what about Habitat for Humanity? They believe that "every person should have a simple, decent house in which to live" and people of all ages help build them. We may never act on Broadway but we can go to our local theatre group and volunteer our time and enthusiasm. (The leader of our local theater, who both directs and acts, is over 80!)

Those youthful dreams, returning to us now that we are old, help us to live the rest of our lives with deeper purpose, meaning and completeness.

MAKING DREAMS COME TRUE
An Exercise in Waking Up To the Past

What an opportunity! Now that you are older, with more time to give to yourself, you can return to your forgotten dreams of long ago. Think back to when you were a little girl, a teenager, a young woman. What did you dream of doing? Tell yourself, with all the unsophistication of that young you, about your dream (or, even better, share this with a friend).

Notice what is happening as you tell yourself your own story. Are you smiling? Are there tears? Does the dream still excite you? Do you still want to do this important thing? Or perhaps you now have a new important dream?

A dream has a factual basis ("I wanted to bicycle alone across America") but it also has its special significance for you ("because I loved the solitude of the wilderness; because I wanted to experience my country and its people in a personal, intimate way; because I was excited by the thought of the long physical exertion it would involve..."). With this in mind take paper and pen, settle down in a quiet place where you can think and ponder and dream, and complete the following:

41

1. When I was young I wanted to. . . . . . because...

2. When I was young I didn't fulfill my dream because... (Check your answer to this. Sometimes we blame other people or circumstances for decisions that were really our own. If you suspect that this is true for you are you going to let that happen again? If so, pay particular attention to the next section.)

3. Now that I am older I want to. . . . . . because...

Now, answer YES or NO to the following statements:

1. Even though I am now... years old, I am still allowing other people and outside circumstances to prevent me from fulfilling my dream.

2. Now that I'm... years old I'm going to make my dream come true.

I'M GOING TO WAKE UP TO THE PAST!

If you have a spouse or companion in your life, do the exercise I describe in the essay "Forgotten Dreams". Before starting this exercise each of you must promise to be completely honest. You must also promise to honor the other's dreams and to do all that is possible to help realize them.

Then go into separate rooms (not just different parts of the same room) and make a list of what you want to do now that you are retired. Give yourself plenty of time to do this. You might want to take several days to think about your list. Then meet when you have quiet time to be together and share your dreams.

It takes courage to do this because what is on these two lists may contain surprises. The desires may seem incompatible (he wants to go and build houses for Habitat while you want to stay at home and learn to paint). Or you both may wish to stay close to home but one has no particular desires to do anything while the other wants to become a minister. Or one may wish to fulfill the dream of parachuting out of a plane while the other feels an unequivocal "No".

It is here that each must remember the promise to honor the other's dream. The task is then to figure out a way to make it happen. Can you each recognize that the dream of the other is important? Can you say, "I can't imagine why anyone would want to paint, (build houses for Habitat, become a minister, jump out of a plane). But I know that this is important for you. Even though I don't want to do it I agree that you need to do it."

It is in such a spirit of acceptance that the seemingly impossible can be worked out. Is it possible to pack the paints and go along to the Habitat site, painting the strange naked beauty of half-built houses instead of the pot of geraniums on the back porch? Is it possible to accompany your partner on the parachuting adventure, observing the process of training so that the thought of your loved one jumping out of a plane is not so alarming? Can you both accept that one will stay at home while the other is active outside? Can you set up specific times when you will be apart and times when you will be together, good times just for the two of you, so that there will be no estrangement?

Women need to be particularly careful in drawing up these plans with a male partner because most of us have been taught to subjugate our own needs to the more "important" needs of husband and family. Has this been true for you? Are you still doing that? As you and your husband face the problem of fulfilling, perhaps, disparate needs, do you find yourself giving up, giving in? Are you, perhaps for the second time in your life, saying good-bye to your dreams because they don't fit in easily with another person's needs? Remember that just as your husband and his dreams are important, so are you and yours.

Finding a way to draw up a plan that includes the dreams of both of you is an important thing to do and not only because it will happily make your dreams come true. It also tells you both that, no matter what happens in the future, you will always be able to find the way of mutual respect, kindness and harmony. Perhaps another dream come true.

Being Alone

LEARNING TO LIVE ALONE

While a couple tries to adapt to the changes that retirement brings they know that one day there will be another change; that eventually one will die and the other be alone. It is difficult to imagine the loss of the loved one with whom so many years have been shared. It is also difficult to contemplate how the one that is left will manage to deal with the everyday responsibilities. There is so much taken care of by one partner that is only vaguely known by the other.

Even in the most egalitarian relationship responsibilities are usually divided; it is simply more efficient to do it that way. We also have natural preferences that point to how the work will be shared. Cultural expectations, too, influence us so that men usually take care of the car and women are responsible for the cooking. So when we look into the future and realize that one partner will one day have to take care of everything, the sadness is coupled with concern. "Will he be able to manage? Will I be able to manage?"

Ideally each partner can teach the other what he or she needs to know, but this is difficult to do. It feels

47

contrived, almost cold-blooded. It seems as if an unnecessary and undesirable intrusion is being forced into a secure and contented relationship. But is it? Looked at another way it can be seen as a most loving and caring thing to do. Each is saying to the other, "I want you to be as safe and comfortable as possible when I am gone so I'm going to show you now what I have been doing all these years."

Much of the information is easy to write down, talk about, and file away: "Every 3,000 miles take the car to the Ace Garage. Here's the phone number. Ask for Bill." That may be important one day. It joins information about banking, insurance, taxes, investments. Many women don't know about these things and need to know.

But in many ways men have more to learn, and more pressing things to learn, than women do for it is women that have traditionally taken care of grocery shopping, cooking, laundry and house cleaning: those tasks basic to daily living. It is here that an interesting and ironic situation exists. For the many years of their working life most men have been free from household tasks. They have gone off to work wearing a clean shirt that magically appeared in the closet. They have returned home confident that dinner would magically appear on the table. Even among younger couples, and even when the wife works outside the home, this is still largely true. Many men "help" but the word "help" implies that housework is the woman's responsibility. Very few couples share the work equally.

It has been suggested that men are able to advance their careers as they do partly because there is a woman in the background seeing that the daily chores get done. Men are free to do other, more "important" things by not having to think about dinner and clean shirts. Most men, in fact, after divorce, remarry quite soon. Is it because they need a wife to do these things for them; things they are unable, or unwilling, to do for themselves? So it seems that men have it made, and women complain about the relentless, daily responsibilities they are expected to assume even when they work outside the home.

But do men really "have it made"? Is this arrangement entirely positive for men? Is it not true that what appears to be their strength is, in fact, also a weakness? Lack of accomplishment in the daily tasks of living makes many men (though, happily, not all) into dependent beings, like children who cannot look after their own basic needs. At no time does this dependency manifest itself more starkly than when a man is left alone in old age. The great void left by the death of his wife is enough to bear. That the house gets dirty and the laundry piles up only adds to the feeling of despair. It is probably not an unrelated fact that the highest suicide rate of any group of people in the United States is that of old men. The rate increases alarmingly as men get older and older. (The rate for old women decreases.) Social scientists have done little research to find out why this should be but I suggest that this unfamiliarity with the minutiae of providing for their own, daily needs may have something to do with it.

There are other differences between women and men as they deal with the housework in their retirement. When a woman gets up in the morning and makes the coffee she does more than just make the coffee. The act is symbolic of assuming responsibility for herself and her family: of running her household. And these are ancient tasks. When we watch a documentary about primitive tribal life we see the women doing what we

49

women still do, in our own way, today. So, when a woman makes that pot of coffee she links herself to all those who have gone before her and done similar things. I see these household responsibilities as supporting for the woman, for they tie her tightly to life and at the end of life they give structure and meaning.

Most women, also, have a long history of doing these things. This means that her later life is a natural continuation of her earlier life. While her role as mother changes, while work outside the home may cease, running the household goes on. This is important. This is what women do. This is what women have always done.

For men it is more difficult. Life spent in the office and factory does not have that earthy bond that ties a man to all men, past and present. Nor is the office, the workshop, carried into the later, retirement years. So for men more than women there is a greater split between life before retirement and life after it. If a man's wife is no longer there to provide his food and comfort this discontinuity is further reinforced and the inability to provide for his own basic needs can result in feelings of helplessness, hopelessness and depression.

So, while the wife needs to learn what her husband does, it is, perhaps, even more important that he learn what she does. And if he can find that he enjoys doing what she has always done then his effort is doubly rewarded.

Retirement and old age are truly times of change. There are major challenges to work out. Time takes care of our fears and tensions as we try to adapt to our new lives, but we must proceed slowly. Retirement itself usually occurs suddenly: literally from one day to the next. But we cannot change our old behaviors and feelings so quickly. Our long life has allowed us to practice what we normally do so that we feel powerful, expert, in control. When learning new tasks we feel awkward, stupid, out of control. It is then that a man may say that as women generally live longer than men it is unlikely that he will have to do these female tasks. That is true, just as it is statistically unlikely that his house will burn down. But he is wise to have fire insurance!

SOLO FLIGHT

The long years of work, family, and marriage are over. Now, perhaps for the first time, life is lived alone. Used to the presence of others, unaccustomed to being with oneself, loneliness enters and with loneliness walks silence: the silence that comes to those who are lost, alone in the deep unfamiliar woods, afraid.

And along with the silence walks time. Time that once was elusive, never enough, now hangs heavy, hangs slow. The fog of slow time silently fills the crevices of living, covering, hiding, obliterating.

Time stops. Sound stops. The body sitting in the chair has forgotten how to live in the old familiar way. Now there is living without life, crying without tears, touching without sensation. Only the shell remains: cracked and dry.

There is silence as she chops the onion, conscious of the years that lie silently in the fog-bound future, chopping other onions for other meals to stay alive for more silence, more slow time, more living without life.

The wedding vows that fashioned those two young people into one "till death do us part" said nothing of the time after the parting when the two who had become one became two again, one gone, one left to live alone this life of heavy silence and slow time. Life has no meaning, for the one who is gone was the meaning. The shared daily round, the shared touch, the shared past, the shared thoughts, gave life to living. Silence was the rest between the notes of the song, slow time the uncurling of a leaf. Blood flowed in the veins.

Loneliness pulls us down to the very bedrock of our existence; of all human existence. If never before, now we are forced to face this creature we call "myself" with whom we have lived so long, so familiar yet so strange. What remains when work, marriage, and family are taken away? What is left when we are left with ourselves?

Being alone is an identity shunned in our culture. Look at TV commercials, look at advertisements. The message is "togetherness": the work group, couples, families, old people with their spouses, an old woman with her daughter. People who spend much time alone are "loners" and the word has negative connotations. A "loner" is seen as an unfortunate thing to be: odd, unfriendly, somehow wrong. An "old loner" is even more unfortunate, an object of pity if anybody bothers to notice.

So it is not only with grief but also with trepidation that we face living alone: trepidation at how we will manage and trepidation at how others will react. There may be a suspicion that the two go together. Those who manage their aloneness well are attractive to others, admired and respected. Those dragged down by their aloneness are pitied, avoided, abandoned.

We see them, those who simply endure their lonely lives. They turn up at appropriate functions, smile, "I'm fine," "I keep busy," then leave, back again to the heavy silence, the slow time. We see them at the supermarket where they go most days just to be close to people, any people. At the check-out stand they say, "Please go ahead. I'm not in a hurry," an opportunity to stay a little longer.

They feel themselves to be outside life, looking in. They are the poor, cold child of the Victorian morality story, standing in the snow, looking through the window into the warm golden room where the fortunate ones eat and talk and laugh. Within that room people live lives of meaning and purpose; lives that are interconnected, interrelated, bound by the bonds of love and mutual responsibility.

During the years of marriage, work, and family, there was a powerful feeling of being right there at the center of that interconnecting web of love and mutual responsibility. Relatedness surrounded us and gave meaning to our life. It was for those others that we worked and planned. It was they who gave us our identity; they were the looking-glass that told us who we were. But now they no longer surround us so no longer tell us who we are. Our sense of self is threatened. We wonder if there is anything within that can live without others to nurture it. We wonder if there is anything within that exists at all.

Perhaps, though, life is handing us exactly what we need if we are to create the life that can be experienced only at this stage in our lifetime. Perhaps we need this slow time and this silence to do the things that must be done. The energy that for so long was directed to familiar others is now diverted into new channels. The web of interconnectedness, reduced to a single damaged thread, is rewoven. Now life is more than the daily round of family and friends. The web of life expands to encompass greater inclusion outside and greater awareness within.

Some welcome the slow time, using it to volunteer for work that interests them and is important. Filling their days with activities, the quiet of their home becomes a welcome, restful reward. Their work has meaning for them. They know that as long as they live in this world they affect it, playing their part in "the endless knot of nature" as Alan Watts called it. To spend three afternoons a week helping a refugee speak English has a result that changes not only the life of the student but, very probably, many other lives as well. Everything we do sends out ripples that affect more than ourselves. To teach English to a struggling young person is an accomplishment greater than it seems. A gift to the future and the world.

Here, then, is one answer to the fear of aloneness: to know that even while we prepare our meal for one and sleep alone in that big bed, we are just as much a part of the universe as we ever were. Here we are, in our later years, expanding our web of life outward so far that it includes places and people we will never know nor need to know.

Others transform their loneliness into solitude. Loneliness longs for time with others. Solitude embraces time away from others.

Here, in solitude, is the long slow time needed to experience nature; here is the silence that allows us to listen again to the world. Thoreau wrote in his book, *Walden*, "Sometimes...I sat in my sunny doorway from sunrise till noon, rapt in a revery, amidst the pines and hickories and sumachs, in undisturbed solitude and stillness, while the birds sang around or flitted noiseless through the house...I grew in those seasons like corn in the night, and they were far better than any work of the hands would have been. They were not time subtracted from my life, but so much over and above my usual allowance....I silently smiled at my incessant good fortune."

Here, now, we can search within to find our deepest feelings and needs, never before expressed and yet, when they appear, half-familiar. We find that they tell us who we really are and perhaps for the first time we get to know ourselves. We start to understand the life we have lived. We realize why some times were so hard and others so joyful. We learn what is important in our lives and in doing so we make decisions about our future. Without knowing ourselves so well we might waste the years that are left. Recognition of our deepest feelings and needs allows us to structure our old age as a time of discovery and fulfillment: the gift that only a lifetime can bring.

Here we find prayer, not as request but as worship, touching the god within so that it might be manifest in our experience of living. Using the time that solitude brings allows us to know, perhaps as never before, that the god within is always there, always our companion, guide and comforter. Here lies reassurance, hope, and strength.

Here we find the goodness we were born with, covered for years by the muck of life, now re-born, clean and true. Now we can put away old hurts and old angers. They were part of the muck that hid our goodness. They have no place in our lives now. The aging years are our time to feel and to show our love: to be kind and to be grateful.

Here, at last, we find the essence of what it is to be human.

I remember a summer evening. Walking along the cliffs near my house, I stopped to watch as the day ended over the ocean. The sun fell, disappeared, the sky blazed then faded leaving the ocean gray, waves hardly visible, sound now taking the foreground of my awareness, the pull, the crash, the tumbling pebbles, again and again and again. There was no moment when it was time to turn and walk on. I could have stood there all night, seen the morning sky, seen the sun rising in a different place, seen eternity. There was no end. There is no end.

And so with our lives. The ones we loved are no longer there but our life, changed, goes on, always part of the emerging moment, always important because it is part of the larger whole.

A story is told about Mahatma Gandhi. As the train he was on pulled out of the station a journalist shouted to him, "What is your message to the people, Mahatma?" With the train gathering speed Gandhi scribbled on a piece of paper and threw it to the man running along beside: "My life is my message."

Now at the end, alone with the time and the silence, we can ask ourselves, "What is the message of my life?" Yes, work, marriage, children, undoubtedly. But is there more? Do the years ahead give us the opportunity to scribble our message and pass it on? For some it will be socially important work; for some it will be more loving relationships with others; for some it will be newly found creativity in art, music, writing; for some it will be a turning inward, searching for a deeper awareness of what it is to be human.

It is in slow time and silence that we find our message and the strength to live it. It will, in its own way, affect the universe as did the lone bird who, unaware, flew low before that setting sun, black against the wine-red sea and caused my heart to leap.

Red Hat Moments

When I was a little girl in England, my Scottish father used to call the last night of the year Old Year's Night. When I came to America I found it was called New Year's. In fact it's a time of looking back and of looking forward. When we are young we have few years to look back on and many to look forward to. Growing old gives us many to look back on and fewer to look forward to.

And this difference is important. Having so much living behind us gives us an opportunity to stop and evaluate. How can I make the most of the years that are left? What do I want to retain? What do I need to change? What can I introduce that is new?

It is this last question that I am thinking about as we move into a new year. I am reminded of two written works. One is that little poem by Jenny Joseph: "When I am an old woman I shall wear purple with a red hat that doesn't go...and run my stick along the public railings and make up for the sobriety of my youth..." In the other, 85-year-old Nadine Stair says, "...Oh, I've had my moments, and if I had it to do over again, I'd have more of them...Just moments, one after another, instead of living so many years ahead of each day."

Yes. That's what I need. More red hat moments. That's what I'll plan for my New Year.

PLEASE TELL ME OLD LIFE IS GOOD LIFE

I'm getting older and I'm not finding any good models," she said. What was she looking for? Reassurance, perhaps. How am I going to be when I am old? What is it like to have wrinkles and, perhaps, failing health, not a lot of money, no longer working, maybe living alone ...? Where are the women that do it well? What does it mean to "do it well"? Will I ever be a model old woman?

Was she also saying that she was frightened? The future seemed uncertain, sad, lonely, death suddenly looming. The years that had passed had rushed by and here she was, unprepared, wishing, perhaps, that she had done things differently, impossible to go back, afraid to go forward into an unknown future.

Will she find her model old woman? Is there such a thing? Is there only one model or are there several to choose from? And must she search for her model "out there" or is it really "in here"? Does she already have, within her, the knowledge, the sense, of whom she wants to be in the years ahead?

But models help. When we were younger and started our first job, got married, had our first child, we noticed how those who were already there behaved: how they looked, what they said, what they did, how they felt about it all. We sought out those we admired and added their characteristics to the picture of how we wanted to be. We noticed some and thought, "I don't want to be like that." Without models we would have had to start from scratch without much idea of where we were going.

A model gives us direction. Several models give us several directions. We observe them, we choose from among them, we accept, we reject, we copy, we experiment, and, eventually, we develop our own style, our own voice. One day we become models for those that come after us.

Searching for models of aging is different from searching for models of being a nurse, a journalist, a mother, for these roles come with some structure. We have an idea of what each of them is supposed to do, what attitudes and values we associate with them. A nurse must have specific knowledge and training, be licensed, efficient, caring and compassionate. And when we find one who fits our expectations we say, "Now there's a good nurse."

But there is no such blueprint for aging and being old. The aged role has been called "the roleless role" because we cannot say what an old person should do and should be as we can say what a nurse should do and should be. It is this lack of identity that is so disconcerting.

It is here that models are useful. They remind us of the alternatives from which we may choose. They give us, in their various examples, advice. We can observe, in a very personal way, the living demonstration of the choices we have to make. Some models push us away ("If I go on feeling sorry for myself I'll end up like that.") others pull us on ("I've always wanted to do that. Why not try? At my age I've got nothing to lose and everything to gain.")

Every old person we meet is a model, for every old person demonstrates his or her particular way of growing old and being old. If we only go out to play Bingo then our models will be limited but we can find models everywhere: selling their fruit and vegetables at the Farmer's Market, sitting in little groups by the wayside painting the scene, learning at Elderhostels, working for political parties, volunteering at hospitals and churches and universities, sitting on committees, taking their daily walk or swim, eating their lunch at the Senior Center. They are in many places if we take the trouble to look for them and if we become involved in activities that allow us to meet them.

We see most of our models, of course, when they are out and doing. These are models for activity and involvement. But the question of how to be old is not only what to do but what to think, what to believe, how to feel about being old. So, perhaps when we look for good models we are not only looking for what to do; maybe we are also looking for reassurance and inspiration. Where is the person that can tell me it's all right, that I am safe, that old life is good life? Where is the person that can show me how to be content and happy and strong in spirit?

I do not know where you or I can find the person we seek though I know that such women exist and if we search we will find. I also know that by asking these questions we have already started to become such a woman. For our model lies within us as well as outside us. Others can show us the alternatives but each one of us makes our own decisions. Somewhere, perhaps buried deep, but waiting, waiting to be recognized, we know how we want to be, we know how we want to be old. If someone shows us that old life is good life it opens a door, gives us a peep at a vision, but the vision is realized only when we recognize it, when we can tell ourselves that, yes, old life is good life. Only then will we set out to make it so. Only then will we find our own unique and idiosyncratic way of living our own good old life. No one can do that for us.

Good life does not just happen. It is not a "thing". It is a conglomerate of many, many decision, many details. We know already what these details are: a balanced, sensible diet, sufficient fluids, daily physical exercise, mental stimulation (getting books from the library, taking a college class, joining a reading or writing group), being involved with others in paid or volunteer work that we enjoy, paying attention to the interests and hobbies of a lifetime, having fun with friends, finding the place where our spiritual needs can be met: these are the components of a good, active, and involved life. And all of these are necessary. We may eat correctly but not exercise, or exercise and then sit in front of mindless television for most of the day. That will not do. We have to decide to do it all.

And then there are the decisions we make about how we feel, for we have a choice about that, too. Being content and happy and strong in spirit is a decision we can make. When a younger person snubs us because we are old (and they sometimes do), we can feel diminished and upset or we can quietly hope that some day this young person will know that old age is the gift of a lifetime. When we look back over our life we can churn up all the old hurts and angers or we can remember the gifts of love and kindness and inspiration that people gave us. When we look into the future we can be consumed with fear that the worst will happen or, knowing that we are arranging our life in a sensible fashion, we can feel confident that we can maintain our steady center to the end. It is just as much our choice how we feel as it is our choice whether we take the trouble to go to the library to find interesting books to read.

It is the choices we make that create our life. Outside models help us along the way but we have to choose to emulate them and choose to do the work that entails. It is only when we ourselves have made these decisions that we can say: "Yes, my old life is going to be a good life."

THE CHRISTMAS GIFT

The family comes to Grandmother's house for Christmas: the hustle and bustle, packages all over the floor, the smell of turkey and pine, the little ones' radiant faces, the support and love of the grown children. The storybook Christmas comes true – for some. But for others Christmas means sadness and loneliness. The children and grandchildren live too far away, a loved husband has died. Christmas becomes the cruelest time of the year.

Must we watch the busy shoppers, hear the Christmas music, see our friends happily making their plans, while we feel only the pain, living again the memories, now bitter in their sweetness, struggling to come to terms with the knowledge that the past is over, that life can never again be the way it used to be?

The better the past the harder it is to accept the present and the future. When we were younger we took for granted that the pleasurable things we did this year would be repeated next year. How unthinkingly we lived with those ongoing relationships, those repeated activities that nurtured love and became family traditions. Most of us were hardly aware of how precious and important they were.

There were changes in our lives when we were younger, too; sometimes upheavals. But when familiar relationships and traditions were disrupted (a different location, a marriage, changes in work), we had the feeling that our life-experience was expanding, that things were getting better. Hope existed in our hearts.

But hope is destroyed when we ache for a time that is no more. Going to the post office, watching the little parcels that should have been under the family tree thrown onto a pile with hundreds of others, buying a sad piece of chicken for Christmas dinner, sitting in church among the suddenly expanded families with their new Christmas sweaters and their new baby grandchildren; these experiences can obliterate hope.

Must Christmas, then, be a time simply to be endured? It will be if we hang on to the way things used to be and expect them now to be the same. If we insist on things being the way they "should" be we will spend that special day feeling deprived and depressed, resentful and angry.

As we grapple with our disturbing memories we may eventually come to understand that the love we experienced in the past is a precious gift, truly a gift of grace. It impels gratitude, not sadness, and with gratitude the experience comes astonishingly alive in us again. We recognize it, we treasure it. The reawakening shows us that we do not have to fear. Love has not gone away. It will never go away even though those who played their part have gone. We do not receive such a priceless gift so that later we may be sad or bitter. We need to nurture the grace of human love so that it can stay warmly alive in our heart. It healed us then, it can heal us now, and it will if we find another way to be loved and to love again. For love not only has personal value, it has universal value. Our love can touch the lives of others. In fact, paradoxically, it is only by giving it away that we keep the love we have known. Our gratitude to those who gave us their love in the past impels us to pass it on. We must not waste that gift of grace.

Thus strengthened we can move on. We can greet the families with their Christmas sweaters and new grandchildren and truly share their pleasure. They will see a person that the years have made loving and kind.

But what can you do on Christmas Day that will nurture the love and warmth you have known? Do you eat your little bit of chicken in front of the television set? Not unless that is what you wish to do. But after all those years of traditional family Christmases, two new Christmas experiences can await you.

One is to invite another, or others who are alone, into your home to share the day. The person who feels sad and angry will see such an arrangement as one sad failure spending time with another sad failure. Who needs that? The person who accepts that a new life awaits will embrace the opportunity to pass love on. Loneliness and isolation are inevitable if we believe that only certain people (family and a few friends) can be close to us and share our lives. When we are able to touch the common humanness we share with everyone we find an infinite variety of relatedness to others. We can all find part of ourselves in another, and from that experience comes wholeness both for ourselves and for the other who shares, however briefly, a moment in our life.

To share Christmas Day in this spirit, with another who would otherwise be alone, to reach out in kindness, with openness of heart, is to make the day an affirming experience, a Christmas gift both to the other and to oneself. It reinforces the warmth of human relationships, learned at Christmases past, now brought into the reality of the present.

Another new experience on Christmas Day is to take your solitary situation as an opportunity. Instead of aloneness being a sad failure, you can see it as a gift, a gift that you give to yourself. Plan your own special day entirely as you wish. What time to get up, what to wear, what to cook, the walk, the church visit, the trees, the birds, when and where to eat, music, reading, writing, drawing: whatever is your own special desire.

I was alone last Christmas. I will never forget it. The solitude became a spiritual experience that will never leave me. By embracing my aloneness its mighty power became revealed to me. I was able to experience the simplest things at a depth and meaning I had never known before. As the three days of solitude passed and I became more able to allow myself to experience the silence, the slow time, the awareness of every moment, texture, color, taste, I realized that here was life, real life. This is what it is all about, I thought. The busy, running, hustling, chattering life that we fall into when others are around is pale in comparison with this.

A Christmas gift comes in many packages. When we are open to the alternatives that the day offers us we give ourselves a gift, a gift that is just right, perfect, tailored for oneself, "personalized" as they say.

It is difficult to allow ourselves to experience deeply something that has always seemed fearful. To enjoy Christmas without the family can seem like a rejection of those absent loved ones. "If I enjoy my Christmas without them what am I saying about my years with them?" we may ask. Only that what we do and what we enjoy this year does not change the integrity and pleasure of past years. There is plenty of love and pleasure to go around. We do not need to ration ourselves. We do not need to make unnecessary sacrifices. Spending a happy day with others or spending it contentedly alone does not take anything away from those warmly remembered days from the past. Instead it offers us the opportunity to recreate the past in a new way in our new life, to be grateful for and to nurture the gift of love we received, and to carry it with us, our needed strength, into the future.

IS LIVING ALONE FOR YOU?

An Exercise in Responding to Life Alone

M any women find themselves living alone as they get older and for those who married right out of school or college this may be a new experience. Because women typically live longer than men it seems inevitable that they will probably spend the last years of life alone though, as we will see, this does not have to be true. What is your experience of living alone?

Take paper and pen, sit quietly, and, thinking about your past, write down your responses to these questions.

1. What did you learn about being alone when you were a child? Did your your parents encourage or discourage aloneness? Do you remember feelings associated with being alone? Does anything else come to mind?

2. Have you had periods of living alone during your life? When? What were they like for you?

73

Look at your responses. You may begin to see that your past has played its part in creating for you facts and feelings about being alone.

Now, respond to these questions:

3. What is it that you like about living alone at the present time? Your answers will refer both to doing and feeling. For example:

    I like: · waking up to a day that's all mine
             · having time to do things without interruption from others
             · cooking when I want to not when I have to

    I feel: · free
             · peaceful
             · happy

4. What is it that you don't like about living alone? For example:

    I don't like: · having no one to talk to
                   · not knowing how to fill up the time
                   · cooking for one

    I don't like feeling: · afraid
                           · lonely
                           · depressed

Look at what you have come up with. What does it tell you about yourself as a person who lives alone? Do you see how your earlier experiences with being alone influence your attitude at this time in your life?

You are fortunate if you thoroughly enjoy living alone. However, as I write elsewhere, living alone can lead to problems if you become sick, disabled or for any reason in need of help and companionship. It is wise, eventually, to live with someone, but because you enjoy your aloneness always make sure you have the time alone that you need.

If you dislike some aspects of living alone and can see that your early experiences created your response, you may realize that it is not living alone that is bad but your response that makes it bad for you. Some people decide to "go against the feeling". They teach themselves to enjoy something they have previously not enjoyed. If we really want to change our responses we can. (I list some books about solitude at the end of this book.)

But maybe you hate living alone and have no desire to like something you dislike! So, instead of trying to change your response, try to change your living arrangements. Remember that the older years are the gift you are given at the end of your lifetime. It is tragic to allow the later years to be lost in sadness, fear and depression. We have the potential for joy no matter how many years we have lived or how short a time we have left. If you are denying yourself the joy that could be yours because of the way you live then you must change your living arrangements. There is no reason why you should be unhappy during this precious time at the end of your life. There are plenty of others now living alone with whom you could share a home. Read "How to Be a Happy Homesharer" and look forward to a new, happier, safer life.

Planning Ahead

THE SILKEN BONDS OF LOVE

I recall a story told to me by a friend. Her mother had said, "If your father goes first, I have arranged to go into a nursing home so I won't be a burden to you." My friend said, "I feel so sad. How could my own mother be a burden? I love her so much. I want to help her if she ever needs me."

What is happening when people say, "She's very kind, but I couldn't possibly be a burden on her"? We are told that loving means giving. But is it possible that loving also means receiving? I think of the little gifts that small children give us: the sticky candy, clutched all the way home in the hot little hand, offered to the mother as a gift of love: the upturned face, flushed and shiny, the sweaty, grubby fingers curled around the damaged, unappetizing, priceless offering. The child loves and gives all she has. The mother receives, and in receiving loves the child and acknowledges her child's love.

But now the mother who received the sticky offering has become the mother unwilling to receive another gift of love offered by the same child. The mother has changed: changed from the gentle mother to the sad, proud, moralistic, tight, withdrawn mother who does not want to be a "burden"; the mother who can no longer love enough to receive love.

What has happened, as the years have passed, to change us, to harden us, to separate us? Why can we no longer allow ourselves to be tied by the silken bonds of love?

I wonder if, during those long years from child-hood to old age, we have accepted the American notion of rugged individualism, pulling oneself up by one's own boot-straps, going it alone, beholden to no one no matter what the cost. Oh, what a glorious, heady, destructive notion! It leads, finally, downward, away from those who want to love and share, down to the lonely, impersonal services of poorly-paid, overworked "health providers", down to life in a narrow bed, in a narrow room, with an unchosen room-mate. Are we more comfortable with paying money than with receiving and giving love? Per-haps, in order to be able to receive offers of help we must see ourselves as having something to offer in return and the only thing an old person thinks she has to offer is money?

Are we controlled by the belief that accepting help means weakness? Is there a desire to hang on to more youthful strength even when that strength has faded away? Are we terrified of becoming the child to the child who becomes the mother? Do we believe that no one, not even one's own child, could love one enough to want to give so much? Or is it that after all the years of being the one that nurtured and helped, we have forgotten how to receive help? After all the years of giving love have we forgotten how to receive it?

The little child with her sticky gift was not think-ing, "Mother does so much for me. She cooks my meals, washes my clothes, drives me to my friend's house. I must give her something in return." Such an idea in the mind of a four-year-old is preposterous. She had not yet learned about exchange. She didn't know that "one good deed deserves another". Because she was only four she was still able to express pure, uncontaminated love. Her gift was not a payment for anything.

It is unthinkable, too, that the mother would have said, "No. I won't take your candy. I'm sure you'd rather have it yourself." What a blow, what an insult, a disappointment, a denial of her child's simple blessing. The mother would never have said such a thing. She knew that to refuse her child's gift was an unloving thing to do. She knew that she wanted to receive the treasure.

Why is it difficult to see that the offer of help now is no different from the offer of candy so long ago? They both come from the same source. The middle-aged child is still holding the gift, still looking into the face of the mother, still saying, "Please. This is for you."

Perhaps, if the mother will sit quietly she will realize how forlorn she feels, how cut off, sad, and lost. She is not happy when she says, "No." She is not smiling. She is not looking forward to her future. Then, perhaps, alone with her thoughts, she will be able to dream of a better future: of herself and her child setting out, in the years that are left, to find another away of showing their love for each other, the same as, and not the same as, the sticky candy love, coming now from a new, richer, more mature, more conscious and expressive awareness: of life and death, of memories and hopes, of the knowledge that can come only from living a life: that loving kindness is all we have and all we need.

And Come Safe Home

So little Jessica was taken from the only home she had known in her short life.[1] The nation asked, "Isn't there a better way?" Every day old people who are not sick are taken from the home that holds a lifetime of memories and "placed" in a nursing home. We have to ask, "Isn't there a better way?"

Some, certainly, need the care that a nursing home offers. Family and friends cannot look after a very sick person. First a hospital and then the care that a really good nursing home provides is needed. But there are old people living in nursing homes who are not in need of skilled medical care on a 24-hour basis. They are frail but they are not sick and it is important to know the difference. They need help with everyday living: bathing, dressing, cooking, shopping, walking, medications. The cost of paying someone to give this help becomes prohibitive. The only answer seems to be a nursing home.

Do you know what that means? It means living for the rest of your life in a room with one or two other people. There need be no more than three feet between the beds, a very small space for clothes and belongings, a bedside table, chair and reading light. That is all. But

---

[1] In 1993, after a long court battle, two-year old Jessica was taken from her adoptive parents and returned to the custody of her biological parents.

we are more than a physical body that needs feeding, watering, and cleaning. We are more than a living organism that needs a bed to lie on and some clothes to cover our body. These things will keep us alive as an animal in the zoo is kept alive, but is this the way we wish to end our days? Are we not more important than that, more precious?

An old person is a container, a vessel, a guardian of the moments that have created that life, and it is in that old person's home, that tiny, priceless spot on this earth, that the moments of that life have been experienced. If a person has lived in a house for many years there is a bond between the person and the place that is palpable in its intimacy.

It is here, in this home, among these so familiar objects, that the memories, the stories, the events of the past are powerfully alive in the present. They exist just as certainly as does the chair, the jug, the book. Our past, remembered, makes sense of our life, allows it to be familiar, known, understood. Our past is there in our home as we pull together the strands of our life and weave them into the cloth of who we are. We must not leave our home before we are ready. The old, though frail, need their spot on this earth. It is an important, unifying part of their lives.

In simpler times the old were cared for, when there was enough food for all, by their families. Today, families may live far away, daughters work in offices; life is not as simple. Families do care about their aged parents but sometimes they find it impossible to give the physical care that is needed. While our standard of living has improved, medical knowledge increased, and we're living longer and longer, the elderly unexpectedly find that they had better look after their own interests if their last years are to have the significance they demand. But if the old person is too frail to live unaided and if the children are unable to help, then what other recourse is there than a nursing home?

I can think of no better way of helping oneself than by sharing one's home. This means that no older person should live alone in a one-bedroom house. The older we get the more we need the extra room so that we can share our home and our lives with others. Then, if we need help it is there.

But this is a most unacceptable notion to most people. It's unAmerican! One must be independent! One must never ask for help!

But sharing a life *is* independence. It is giving as well as receiving, helping as well as being helped, nurturing and being nurtured. It offers sociability as well as privacy, conversation as well as silence, shared activities as well as solitary ones. We need all these things, and never as much as when our aging bodies may force us to go more slowly. Two or three living together can flourish when one, alone, cannot. Tasks can be shared, costs are cut. There is more safety and security. Living with others can make the difference between staying at home and going into a nursing home where one is truly dependent.

This is the "better way" we seek. This is how we stay at home when we do not need 24-hour nursing care. This is our freedom. When I see someone who is old taken, unwillingly, away from their home, I grieve for the lack of respect for that long life. It is only when we recognize the importance of the later years that we will seek and find the better way.

I'm Afraid I'll Be a Bag Lady

They are not joking. It's real and it's terrifying. I hear it more and more, from women of 55, 60, 65 who look the future in the face and see no money, no shelter, no food, no dignity, things getting worse and worse until...what?

Some of these women look back on their lives with bittersweet regret. They know they didn't conform. They didn't stay married, they didn't work and save, work and save. They "stopped to smell the roses". They were the grasshoppers not the ants. Looking back they don't regret the quality of their lives. They have wonderful and important memories. They allowed the world to touch them and they touched the world. It is when they look to the future that they wonder if they lived their lives in the best way.

Other women are angry. They did the "right" things. Sometimes, through death or divorce, they raised children alone, hard years, hard work, barely enough to get by on. But they did what they had to do. Sometimes they gave their small savings to a child to help with college or for the down-payment on a house. And now, though they have worked all their lives and been good mothers, they have nothing as they face their old age.

For all these women, ants as well as grasshoppers, the future is frightening. Just a tiny Social Security check.

Not enough to support life now, even less in the future. The poor, who earn little though they work hard all their lives, are entitled to little when they have to stop working. The rich, who earn a great deal when they work hard all their lives, are entitled to much more when they stop working. On the surface it is fair. The more you put in the more you get out: the slot-machine approach to justice. But we are talking of human beings, not candy bars. Was the poor woman's work less valuable just because she could earn so little? Was she less valuable? And what about raising her children, her unpaid work? Is that of so little value that she should suffer in her old age with a Social Security check of $400 a month?

We can shrug it off. She will manage somehow. She will disappear into the shadows. We will not know how she spends her days, her nights, when she feels hungry, when she feels cold, when she feels despair. She will hang on to her house and then her room. Her fear will be the streets, the bag lady. One day she will die. We will not know.

This is the dark side of old age. It is easy to see these years as a precious gift when you have money in your purse, food on the table; when you can afford the price of coffee with a friend, a movie; when you can get to the library, the college, the church and walk safely in the streets. Then you can savor the years, realize your freedom, expand the consciousness of being alive. But for too many old age is a time of restriction rather than expansion.

Once it was possible to live with little money. In rural America, two hundred years ago, the family produced for itself most of what it needed and the old were part of that self-supporting system. But today we can no longer produce what we need. If you live in a city you cannot grow your own food, keep a few chickens, chop your own wood. We are part of a money-for-goods system. We are a nation of consumers, not producers. We have to have money in order to live, and when the old, who have worked hard all their lives, have so little money, their lives are tragic.

In a perfect social system this would not happen. A life of honest labor would be rewarded with enough for dignity and security in old age. We would not see some with far more than they need and more with so pitifully little. But we do not live in a perfect society and few, through the ages, ever have.

Poverty degrades the human spirit. "You cannot buy happiness," say those who have never been poor. They are right if they are thinking of those with money who believe they can find happiness by buying more things: a house, a cruise, jewelry, another car. Once the initial flurry of pleasure has faded they are as discontented as before.

But money, when it prevents deprivation, does buy some happiness. Enough money prevents hunger; it prevents being too cold in winter, too hot in summer; dirty clothes and dirty bed-linen because there is no money for hot water and soap; sickness because there is no money for doctors' fees and medicine.

When people think about poverty it is these physical things they think about: the hunger, the cold, the sickness. We rarely hear about the way poverty grinds down the spirit, destroys joy, pride, the contentment of being alive. People who have never been poor know nothing about the worry, the monotony, the lack of stimulation, the fear and despair. And there is something else. We live in a society that values success, achievement and wealth, and so we value people who are successful and wealthy. There is, as a result, a hidden blaming of those who are poor; they didn't achieve as they should; they are to blame for their condition. And so, for the poor, there is not only the physical deprivation, the worry and the fear, but also the shame.

We hear about the old woman who eats cat food. We secretly wonder what cat food tastes like but we're not going to try a little bit to find out. Does she put it on a plate or eat it straight out of the can we wonder? The physical repulsion dominates our imagination. We don't think about the mental and spiritual anguish she must experience as well. Do the tears fall as she eats her cat-food supper?

It seems woefully inadequate to say that all the aged poor can do is to hang together, but that is probably all that can be done. If power is the ability to control events, then the aged poor can best control the events of their lives by sharing their lives with others. Two can live more cheaply than one and three cheaper still: a simple truth but so hard to accept and then act upon. It is astonishing that, at the end of life, when we are most likely to be in need of companionship, physical help and financial sharing, so many people live alone. In a crisis it can be this lack of support that leads to tragedy. The bag lady might not be on the streets if she had a friend to share a home. The simplest home will do. We don't need much to be safe and free.

So, to quiet the fear of becoming a bag lady, it may be necessary to face a different challenge: living and sharing with others. In the end that is probably the choice and what a choice it can be! To do it well needs all the maturity, patience and thoughtfulness that, for most, only a lifetime can give. For those who wish to improve their lives it can be another rewarding experience.

THE UNKNOWN YEARS

It's a question we eventually face: how and where shall we spend the years that are left now that our children are living their own lives, we have no husband, we are alone? We may, somewhere, have a loving, caring family, we may have good friends, but we have joined that ever-increasing group of people who live in what the Census Bureau calls one-person households.

The years of day-to-day, face-to-face involvement with others in childhood, in college, at work, in marriage, with our children, have come to their end. Gradually, imperceptibly, those absorbing relationships have changed, have slipped away. The day has come when we enter our house, close the door and know we are alone.

Closing the door shuts out the world so being alone is, first, a physical experience. The house is quiet. The furniture, the pictures, the books, sit, waiting, familiar, sharing memories of a noisy, active past, moving, silently now, into the future. Only the refrigerator occasionally surges.

Peace and quiet. The quiet we dreamed of during the racket of our earlier life. The time to go at a new pace, to do exactly what we want to do when we want to do it, get up, go to bed, come in, go out...

Eventually, though, we find we need balance. Time

to be alone but also time to share everyday life with another. Time to bring more human energy into the room, to wake up the furniture, the pictures, the books, to use the things in the house, to talk to a friend, to laugh, to cry, to animate the silence.

But being alone is more than just physical aloneness. Being alone is having to take sole responsibility for every moment of every day of living. Sometimes it is tiresome. Sometimes there may be things we cannot do or do not wish to do. Then we face the time-consuming and expensive task of bringing help into the home from outside.

Being alone is also expensive. Running a house for one is wasteful at a time when we do not have money to waste.

For many the awareness that one is alone marks a great transition, the end that is a beginning, the beginning of the years that lead to the end. How many years we do not know. What they hold for us we do not know. Their secret is hidden from us now: it will be revealed, day by day. Only time can make our personal story clear. Only at the end will we be able to say, "Yes. This has been my life."

So we need to prepare, as well as we are able, for the unknown years. What will we need as we journey on? We know that the years ahead are important and that our home life needs to be supportive of the challenges we may face. Each one of us will have a personal response to what constitutes a supportive environment but there do seem to be certain basic human needs that we all share, needs that were naturally met in our ordinary family life. When we are old and alone we have to look at them again, searching for a way to make sure we do not find ourselves without those basic human needs.

I think of money, of safety, and of companionship.

Perhaps these three are basic to a good life.

But how can one have enough money when demonstrably one does not? We know that when we cannot increase our income we must decrease our expenses but for some this seems impossible. There are certain things one must have in order to exist at all. These expenses cannot be decreased even though they use up all of, and sometimes more than, one's income. But there is a way to achieve the seemingly impossible: by sharing a home and a life with others. Two can live more cheaply than one, and three cheaper still. Many of the old live in houses that are now too large. They have room to share with others. Many live in housing that is sadly inadequate. Together two or three can find a more pleasant and spacious place to make their home.

It costs no more to heat a room when two sit in it than when one sits alone, no more to bake lots of potatoes, to have a telephone or television that several use, to water the garden that two make beautiful rather than one who works alone. Financially, shared living has to help. It can only decrease each person's expenses. And, magically, with this sharing, the other two needs, safety and companionship, can also be fulfilled.

By safety I do not mean only safety from crime, though the extra shared money may mean living in a safer neighborhood. Safety is also the experience of being nurtured, knowing that our well-being is seen as important by another, that we are not dealing with everything by ourselves, but that someone is there: someone to call the doctor if we fall, someone to make the dinner if we are tired, someone to share our laughter, someone to talk to when we are worried or unhappy, someone to soften the alarms of life. And this, of course, is what companionship is all about.

Living alone, when old, especially without enough money to live decently, is an invitation to disaster. It is the lonely poor who, when unable to support the everyday demands of living, find themselves in a nursing home though not in need of 24-hour nursing care. It is they who spend the remainder of their life lying in a narrow bed, less and less able with each passing day to walk about and move around, losing touch with the world outside and eventually losing touch with themselves.

But even though this is what so many people fear, it is hard to take the step that will lead to sharing a home and a life. For we know, sadly, that, while finances and safety can only be improved when we share, it is, as always, the human factor that we fear. The risk of making such a profound change in one's life seems dangerous, impossible, for with whom can we happily share our home and our life?

And certainly there is good reason to arrange a new life carefully. We must know the other person very well indeed for he or she will be our companion for many years. A few trial meals or outings will not do. We don't get to know each other's foibles and irritating habits, we're too much on our best behavior.

What we need is to experience each other in a variety of situations: to see each other at our worst! The car breaking down in the rain, the evening out when everything goes wrong, the day when there is nothing much to do and both feel bored and grumpy; it is situations like these that tell us what we need to know about the other and about ourselves. Is the other person kind, unselfish, humorous, generous, honest, interesting? And are we? "What do I offer?" we must ask ourselves, for if we cannot share burdens as well as pleasures, then the rest of our life is not to be spent with others.

Ideally we will start to share our life with others before we reach a crisis. Then we can experiment with our new life together at leisure, testing for a considerable length of time before taking the plunge, being sure that we truly know each other, that we can trust each other, and that life together is going to be better than life alone.

At the end of Ingmar Bergman's great film, *Fanny and Alexander,* the Uncle, at the christening dinner, proposes a toast to the two babies. I, sitting in the audience, aware that Bergman had announced this would be his last film, suddenly realized that I was about to hear his final message to the world. After all those years of sitting through his difficult and rewarding films I was to be given the wisdom of his lifetime.

And what was that wisdom? When the rhetoric was distilled what the Uncle told the babies, and Bergman told us was, "Be kind to one another." That was it: be kind. And that, I realized, was enough. For kindness includes all the rest: being generous, loving, helping, sacrificing, nurturing.

Imagine. Imagine yourself sharing a home and a life with others. Imagine the rewards and satisfactions and pleasures. Imagine the sacrifices, the disappointments, the bad times. Are you willing? Are you worthy of such an adventure? Are you kind enough?

How to Be a Happy-House-Sharer
An Exercise in Finding the Friend
Who Will Share Your Life

T he very best time to start looking for a house-sharing partner is when you don't need one. You need time, lots and lots of time, to meet a great many people, to come to understand the decisions that have to be made, to realize the adaptations you will have to make as well as the rewards the arrangement will offer, to find out as much as possible about this new adventure. You plan to be living with this person for the rest of the life of one of you. So go slow, take care, but start your search right away.

Searching

If you are not fortunate enough to have a lifelong friend with whom to share, you will have to find your partner. This means being actively involved in searching everywhere for her (or him). Do the things you enjoy doing, go to everything you're invited to, venture into things you have never done before, and talk. Talk to lots and lots and lots of people and when someone seems appealing suggest you meet for coffee or whatever is right for you.

You can also look at ads in the newspaper, and put your own ad in your church bulletin, on your Senior Center notice board. These are the months of searching in an unhurried way. It should be an enjoyable, interesting experience as long as you are not anxious if the right person does not immediately appear. You won't know if you have found the right person for many months yet.

Getting to know a stranger.

Before you can be house-sharers you need to be friends. This is the most important thing I can tell you. In fact, you may not wish to talk about house-sharing at all but just let friendships develop. Be sure you do things together (movies, going to the library and talks and concerts, camping, hiking, sharing hobbies etc.) This allows you to get to know each other in important ways: not only what each of you likes to do but how you respond to situations, who you are. You get to know the dimensions of the other's personality and how it fits with yours. You should also get to know your friend's family and watch how they interact. It is important that they like you and support the arrangements you are making.

As the months go by and you look at the people you are spending your time with you will start to ponder:

- With whom do I feel happy?
- With whom do I feel safe?
- With whom does my life expand in enjoyable ways?
- With whom could I spend many years in the intimacy of a shared household?

Talking about sharing your lives.

Eventually (and do not be surprised if the search takes many months, a year, whatever is necessary) you and your friend will start talking about sharing your home and your lives and immediately a host of things have to be considered. Will one of you move in with the other or will you both start anew in another house or apartment? The latter is better but may not be possible. Details about shared costs, furniture, cooking, pets, visitors and so on will be thought about. Being good friends already gives you the basis that you need at this stage. You will be able to be honest about your own needs while considerate of your companion's needs as well.

Practicing.

When the details seem to be worked out, STOP. You must now spend at least two weeks together in your shared home. No matter how well you know each other you don't know what it is like to share the intimate details of living in the same house. We all have our idiosyncratic ways of being in our own home. Now is the time to be honest about anything that concerns you. It is also the time to compromise. Life is rarely as we imagine it will be. No two people do things in exactly the same way so each has to make little adjustments. Realize that it doesn't matter if you don't wash the dishes, cook, handle money or relate to your children in the same way. Let the other be who she is. Enjoy your differences. What does matter is the overall spirit in the house, the feeling between you of caring, of trust, of enjoyment, of shared interests, of the dedication to make this new adventure work.

Moving in.

At last you are with the friend who will share your life. You cannot know what the future holds. It will sometimes be difficult. Whether or not it will be good depends on your shared commitment both to each other and to your life together. I wish you well.

Feeling Good

WINTER BEAUTY

I once saw a woman, old, wrinkled, beautiful. I had gone to some outdoor event on a hot, summer day, and there she was, sitting on a chair on the grass. Others stood and sat around her. She wore a long cotton dress in a deep, rich color. Her gray hair was pulled back, her face wrinkled, her old hands lay in her lap. She spoke, she laughed, the conversation flowed.

The others were younger. The authenticity of her being as an old woman made the others look too young. Out of them all only she was the right age. Someday the others might, happily, achieve that right age.

I do not know who she was. I never spoke to her. I watched her for a few minutes and then moved on, but the memory of that woman has never left me. I do not know if she had "good bones" or beautiful eyes. That did not matter. Her beauty came from her acceptance of being exactly who she was. Unaffected, simple, her spirit glowed.

Being old means looking old; a great sorrow for many women. Even the young woman, the twenty-five-year old, peers intensely for the tell-tale signs around the eyes, the mirror held so close that it seems she would push right into it to reassure herself that a few more years of youth and beauty remain. Thirty-year-olds are choosing plastic surgery, taking early control against the incipient sag, the potential wrinkle: Aphrodite holding back the tides of time.

Youth jumps at us, loud and insistent, from the billboard, the screen, the magazine cover. Always a new crop of smooth skin and firm flesh while the watching woman, the old crop, sees herself falling further and further behind that fleeting, tantalizing moment of perfection.

On television everyone is young and beautiful. Even the "mature" woman looks oddly youthful. The products sold to us to improve our look are demonstrated by those who are already improved. The commercials show us the beautiful woman in the beautiful robe, patting, oh so gently, the priceless unguent on to her perfect, flawless face. The advertisements for fitness equipment imply that they are to be used only by those already slim and firm. Anyone less than perfect is hidden. The out-of-shape, the blemished are nowhere to be seen. The old woman, scarred by the years of living, is an embarrassment, a cruel joke that lies in wait for these perfect young beauties.

But watching the woman on the grass I learned that beauty is not looking beautiful. Beauty is being beautiful. Beauty is experiencing oneself as right, as the way one should be. Beauty in an old woman lies in her enjoying the way she looks at the age she is. "Here I am. I make no apology for being an old woman, of looking as I do. I've had to live a long time, to do a lot of things, to feel a lot of feelings, before I could look like this. I'm proud of what I've become. One day you young people may finally achieve this look as well."

When we agonize over our aging skin, our wrinkles, the lines on our faces, our scraggly necks, our thinning hair, our thickening waists, our blemished hands, we prevent ourselves from being beautiful for we are concentrating on the wrong things. It is our self-consciousness, our shame, our denial, our despair, that prevents us from being beautiful. What others see is our lack of acceptance of who we are. It is the apologies we make for looking the way we do that make us "old and ugly".

Beauty requires a change of attitude, not a change of skin. Beauty is enjoying one's age, accepting and liking one's look, being proud of receiving the gift of age. When we are able to experience our age as a gift, then others will know that we are important, and beautiful as well.

CAN YOU LOVE YOUR WRINKLES?
An Exercise in Being Beautiful

When everything around you tells you that you can't be both beautiful and old it is very hard to accept the way you look. It is only natural to compare yourself with younger women or with yourself when you were young. You do it even though you know how self-defeating it is: you make yourself feel worse by comparing yourself with someone you can never be.

I find it helpful to look, to really look, at women my own age; just women I happen to know or unknown women I see as I go about my daily business. I am reassured when I see an older woman whose spirit shows in the elegant, well-groomed way she dresses and the confidence with which she holds her body. I smile at another who, without embarrassment, seems to be letting it "all hang out". Watching older women gives me a real feeling of sisterhood with them. Those who seem comfortable and happy with the way they look (no matter what that may be) have something to teach me. Try this yourself. Watch other women and see what you learn. Some signal their acceptance of age. What do you see that lets you know that? Others signal their shame at being old. What is it that sends that signal? Is it the way they hold their body, is it their clothes, is it the way they don't look you in the eye? What signals do you send?

We often have exaggeratedly negative impressions of our own bodies. Do you? Try this. First, find your notebook and pen. Then, taking them with you, stand naked in front of your full-length mirror. Really look at yourself. Maybe you haven't done this for years. What do you see? Now make two columns in your notebook: "What I Like" in one column and "What I Wish I Could Change" in the other. Write down what you see.

You may find it difficult to be honest about "What I Like". Let yourself appreciate yourself. You know if you have beautiful eyes or fine long legs. Write it down. Spend some time on this, searching for things, even little things, that you like. There may be things that nobody else would even notice. But *you* notice them. Write them down.

Now, can you move into the "What I Like" column some of the things you have written in the other column? For example, I really like my hands, not because they have ever been beautiful but because they've done so much for me. They carry the blueprint of my life. They are real, authentic; they tell me a lot about myself; they are my old and precious friends. I don't care about the spots and the scars and their "old look". I love them. If you have included your hands in the "What I Want To Change" column, look at them now. Think about where you've been together; think about what they've done for you. Examine the scars. Remember what happened to give your hands those scars. Can you move them into the "What I Like" column? Can you do this with any other part of your body?

You may have written something in the "What I Want To Change" column that you really hate and can't change. Wrinkles, for example. So, try this. Write "wrinkles" in the "What I Like" column! Yes, I know you don't want to, but try it anyway. It's quite a shock, isn't it, to consider liking your wrinkles when you were quite sure that you don't! How does it feel? Take a hand mirror and look at your wrinkled face. Stroke it, talk to it, talk to your wrinkles, tell them who you got them from (your mother? your father?), talk about that person, tell them you accept them as your family heritage, tell them you are going to wear them proudly.

Is there anything else you can move into the "What I Like" column?

You may want to change your weight, the way your hair looks, things that you can and perhaps need to do something about. Sometimes it takes time to reach a long-term goal like losing weight and it becomes difficult to maintain that early enthusiasm. I find it's helpful to have some sort of physical prop or a model. For instance, can you draw the way you are going to look when you have reached your goal? You can keep your drawing pinned up somewhere to remind yourself. Or write a little description of what you are going to do and what you will eventually look like. Keep it in your bedside table drawer. Remember to read it and make notes on your progress once a week.

Another way to help yourself is to look around for a woman who can become your living model. "Yes, I would like to look like that," you say. Really look at her. What is it about her that is right for you? Sometimes it is not so much a matter of physical attributes as a manner, a spirit, an essence. The woman I saw at the picnic became both a physical and a spiritual model for me. Search for her. She exists. You will find her.

What about the way you dress? A lot of women get stuck with a look that was right for them thirty or forty years ago but is not right now. When we are older we don't have to wear clothes that emphasize our spreading waists. Take a day all to yourself. Go and try on clothes and colors that you have never dreamed of wearing. And don't forget hats. Consignment shops and good thrift shops are great places to experiment. Remember that getting older means being free to do exactly what you want to do: including being a bit eccentric! And what about your hair? Hairdressers (who are usually young) love to cut the hair of older women short. But short hair can be cruel to an aging face and neck. Experiment and tell them exactly what you want.

As you do these little exercises a change will come about. You will realize that you are changing not only your physical appearance but also your feelings about yourself. You are feeling better about the way you look and also about being an old woman. And that is Winter Beauty.

TAKE HEART
Thoughts on St. Valentine's Day

February, that unlikely month for love. One might think that April would be a more suitable month to experience Cupid's arrow. But St. Valentine, the patron saint of lovers, was martyred, so the story goes, in February, so it is in this month that we send our gifts of love.

Perhaps we older people can take heart from this ancient custom for it tells us that love blooms when it will. It knows no restriction from the month of the year or the age of the lover.

Younger people do not know this. They see romantic love as the prerogative of those years when the sap is rising, the flesh is firm and hearts are light. They tend to see romantic love between the old as funny, ridiculous, or even disgusting. It is not unknown for an older person to renounce a desired new marriage because grown children think it shocking. Old people themselves may just assume that the days of romance are over.

But love has nothing to do with the color of hair or the wrinkles on a face. Love is that miracle of delight and compassion and empathy and excitement for another that is as powerful in age as it was in youth. Perhaps, in fact, it is more powerful, for the old have a whole life to weave into their love. As Elizabeth Barrett Browning wrote in her great sonnet, "How do I love thee?": "I love thee with the breath, smiles, tears, of all my life!"

Thank you, St. Valentine, for reminding us.

HOW DO I LOVE THEE?

With this body I thee worship." The ancient words, repeated by the young, carry a strange message into the marriage vows. Experiencing the sexual urgency of their new-found love, "worship" does not seem the right word to describe the hot excitement of sexual attraction, the delights of lusty, urgent, physical passion. Certainly, in modern America, the idea of worship has no place in the narrow concept of "have sex". What a horrible term that is! Have sex, have breakfast. Devoid of romance, wonder, gentleness, passion: the glorious sexual force reduced to mere rutting, the stuff of statistics.

No wonder we do not know what to do about our sexual feelings when the urgency of youthful passion changes to a slower pace; less active, less goal-directed. Taught only to "have sex" we have forgotten about worship. We may never have known that our sexual experience could include esteem, respect and awe.

And perhaps that is hard to do when lives have not been lived long, when a man and a woman have few shared years together. Perhaps the esteem, the respect and the awe come only when the partners have lived much and shared much: the day after day after day after day, each contributing to the mysterious creation we call marriage. To look at one's spouse as life turns toward its end is to look with the eyes of all the years. Contained in the seeing are the thousands of other times one has seen that person. The past cannot be removed from the present.

Now we have reached the time to say thank you for the years, to humbly acknowledge the beloved. It is, perhaps, the awareness that time left together is finite, less every day, that brings us face to face with what needs to be said, what needs to be done. And it is here that we move into that mysterious area of human experience where we find that sexual closeness cannot be separated from the rest of life.

For how else can one tell the other of the richness of a long life together? Words spoken across the dinner table, walking round the lake, driving home from the movies, tell some of the shared story, but words are not enough, gifts are not enough for such intimate expression. When we are at our most expressive we seem to want to touch, we need to touch in fact, for touching is part of the message. Words are too intellectual without that softening influence. The expression of deep respect and gratitude includes the gentle touch, the mystical experience of awe as the fingers feel the face of the beloved, explore the body of the long years' partner, of the one who stood by, who shared the lusty passion and now shares the gentler but equally powerful expression of sexual worship.

They say that the most important sexual organ is our skin. We know this when we allow ourselves the long luxurious time of holding, stroking, cuddling, passion rising when it will, if it will, allowing the feelings to flow unmonitored, uncritically, no records to break, just continuing together the familiar sexual experience with the exquisite intensity that can come only with so many years of living.

Expression of affection, gratitude, admiration, tenderness, contains not only loving words and deeds but sexual love as well. Then the power of the experience, coming as life together moves into its fullness, reveals a sacred quality that gives meaning to the word "worship".

GENTLE STEPS TO SEXUAL WORSHIP
An Exercise in Human Sexual Love

Human sexual love does not start when you get into bed. The first faint stirrings of sexual expression can begin, if we allow them, at any moment in the life we live with our partner.

If the expression of sexual feelings in your relationship flickers faintly or seems to be lost, the first step is to wish it to return. The wish is not only for the fulfillment of your normal sexual urge but for the warm closeness of shared sexual expression as part of your life together. Imagine your life containing again this secret delight with your partner.

But how can this sexual closeness happen? If sexual expression has been weak or non-existent for some time, if it has been an embarrassment or the setting of anger and blame because of physical problems with intercourse, how can it be rekindled?

You need to take the second step: to recognize that satisfying sexual expressiveness does not have to include full genital intercourse. If that happens in a natural, unforced way, then it happens. If it does not, then it does not. There is no judgment, no expectation, no evaluation of the experience. You are not taking a test! You do not pass or fail. You simply experience what you experience. And being older, less urgent, more relaxed, gives you an opportunity to experience your sexual self and your partner's sexual self in new ways.

At this stage you may not wish to talk about this with your partner. You may feel embarrassed or, because of past problems you may fear that your partner will respond in a negative way. You realize how easy it would be to destroy the faint, fragile sexual stirrings that you hope still remain with you both. So, take the third step. Decide to start alone.

The decision to take responsibility for rekindling your shared sexual life leads you to the fourth step: just look at your partner as he does ordinary, everyday things. There he is, in his old, shabby bath-robe, with his newspaper and his cup of tea. You've seen him there so often that you hardly notice him any more. This time, look. Just look. Let his presence enter your heart. Experience the person who has shared the years of your life. Allow the feelings of gratitude and admiration and respect and tenderness hold you as you watch that so familiar figure. If you have never done this before you may find it to be an overwhelming experience.

Now, at step five, express those feelings. Just gently. When he puts away his paper, go close. "I was watching you. How precious you are to me." Say the words that come naturally to you. Not a lot. Just a few. And a touch, a stroke, a meeting of the eyes, whatever is right for you. That's all. No more. But the atmosphere between you changes. The few words, the tiny physical connection introduces a dimension to your relatedness that may have been lost for a long time.

At step six, remain conscious of the other as the days go by. Concentrate on your appreciation. Be gentle in your heart. There is plenty in your partner to love. Speak it, just a little. Touch, just a little.

What you will find, at step seven, is that your partner will respond. We all need affection and appreciation in both words and touch. We all bloom when another, gently, without demands, expresses love. And so a time will come when step eight naturally unfolds. Without embarrassment, without anger or rejection, without any of what may have been those old responses, you start to share time with each other: private time, intimate time, sexual time growing out of the gentle shared expression of gratitude and love.

The words, the reminiscences, the tears, the laughter, the acknowledged future parting, are nurtured by the physical closeness, the touching, the stroking, the sexually reassuring presence. Where you go on your sexual journey will be different at different times: sometimes passionate, sometimes slow and sweet. Perhaps, only now the marriage vow of "With this body I thee worship" will be understood.

Taking Care

Beware False Gods

ecause I had a ringing in my ear that didn't go away I went to see a specialist. I arrived early at his new, beige, impersonal office, for I needed time to complete the forms the receptionist gave me. Lying on top of the pile, the first thing I was being asked to attend to, more important apparently than my medical history, was a request that I sign my consent to binding arbitration in the event of possible legal action. I signed. I felt uneasy.

The young doctor did not look at me when he introduced himself. I told him about the ringing in my ear. He didn't know what it could be. He told me to go for some tests. He said it might need surgery.

At home I tore up the forms for the testing and called someone I had heard about; an M.D. who practiced herbal medicine and acupuncture. Her office was in a little house. Trees grew closely around. The rooms were small and cozy; music played softly; interesting things hung on the walls; I experienced a sense of peace. The doctor smiled at me as she greeted me. I felt her acceptance and interest. I told her about the ringing in my ear and she asked if I had any congestion. "Yes, I do feel stuffed up in the morning." "You probably have some fluid in your inner ear," she said. She gave me pills made in China, the smallest pills I had ever seen, perfectly round. If I dropped one it rolled about the floor, under the bed, got lost in the rug. I learned to be careful. In three days the ringing had gone.

What was going on? Why were my two experiences so different? I looked in my Webster's dictionary to find out where the words come from that we associate with the work that doctors do. "To cure" comes from the Latin "cura", meaning care, concern, sorrow. "To heal" comes from the Anglo-Saxon "hal" meaning whole. "Whole" is defined as complete, not divided up. "To care for" means both "to love or like" and "to look after".

I began to see the picture. I noticed that there were no "medical" or even "physical" words here. I saw instead that the patient (from Old French "to suffer") is sorrowful, is not whole, is divided. The healer loves or likes the patient, is concerned for her, makes her complete again.

Does your doctor love you or even like you? Is he or she concerned about you? Do you feel yourself moving toward wholeness when you are in your doctor's presence?

I think of those television commercials for medical insurance, for home nursing care, for pharmaceuticals. They always reflect caring, loving concern; everything that those ancient words imply. The scene is quiet, the caregivers (there's that word again) kind. They look at the patient lovingly with eyes that are soft and full of compassion, their hands touch the suffering person gently. Their actions are slow, they have plenty of time for their patient. There is a powerful impression of being nurtured, taken care of, made whole again.

Advertisers are clever people. They study the market to find out what we want to buy so that they can sell it to us. And when you study those advertisements it's very clear what we want. We are seeking reassurance, kindness, understanding, compassion. The (usually) male physician may be seen in the background with his white coat and stethoscope (the symbol of medical expertise) but in the foreground is the nurturing caregiver (usually, interestingly, a woman). So the advertisers sell expertise, but most importantly they sell compassion, for we need the soft compassion just as much, or even more than we need the expertise. And studies show that the expression of caring concern and interest, of having the time to talk, to share, to touch, is as important to healing as is the pill, the knife, or the laser.

While some have found a physician that understands this (and I know these physicians are much sought after, as mine is), there is a new realization that too many doctors are unaware, unable, or unwilling to be the concerned healer as well as the skilled technician. The large and growing literature on holistic medicine demonstrates a dissatisfaction with doctors who are only technicians.

In ancient times, and still now in some places, healing was part of religious practice. Sickness was seen as the expression of powerful supernatural forces with which the healer must battle. Even up to the nineteenth century knowledge about disease was so limited that there was little a physician could do for the patient in terms of medicine. What they practiced was art rather than science. The laying on of hands or, as it is now called, the healing touch, could make the patient feel better. When Jesus laid his hands on the sick the spiritual blessing flowed from him to the suffering person. This is not the quick touch of inquiry about lumps and bumps, but the touch that binds the healer and the healed.

The twentieth century has brought vast developments in medical practice. Medical schools teach the science of medicine, the mechanics of medicine, very well, but somewhere the art of healing, the laying on of hands, the caring, the making whole again, is getting lost.

We want our doctors to be two things: first-class technicians and compassionate healers. The wisdom of the advertisement industry implies that perhaps we need the compassionate healer more than the skilled technician. The physician, however, often as a result of his or her training, is all too often only the technician.

Perhaps this is why, after a visit to the doctor, we so often walk away feeling vaguely dissatisfied, feeling there should have been something more though it's hard to know what. We feel constrained in some way. A serious matter of health is being addressed but we find it difficult to be fully open and honest. And we suspect that is true of the doctor as well. What is really going on in his head? Why doesn't he look me in the eye? Why doesn't he give me more time? Why is it all so tight?

It is common wisdom that Americans treat their doctors like gods. But what sort of gods? Benevolent gods? Powerful gods? Punishing gods? Perhaps our metaphor of doctors as gods goes back to those ancient times when the healer battled supernatural forces; when sickness was not a matter of the physical body but a matter of good and evil. If our doctors are to be gods then they must learn to bless us; to lay their hands on us; to re-create us, the suffering ones; to make us whole again.

And it is up to us to choose our gods wisely. Into whose hands are we putting our health, our life, our death, our experience of wholeness and well-being? "Does this physician have wisdom as well as knowledge, kindness as well as expertise?" we must ask ourselves. If not, we need to search for the one who is himself whole, for only he who knows that the body is not separate from either the mind or the soul can help the patient become complete again. We must not accept less.

FINDING A DOCTOR
WHO IS RIGHT FOR YOU
An Exercise in Feeling Better

L
ike many people today, you don't know what to
do. "Where can I get good medical care?" you are
asking and there's a panicky feeling that good
care is increasingly difficult to find. "What will happen
to me if I get really sick and haven't found a doctor I
trust and like?"

In order to find the doctor who is right for you,
you have to believe that person exists. You also have to
believe that you are a good patient for it's important to
acknowledge that the responsibilities go two ways. This
exercise may help you find that good doctor and be that
good patient.

Ask yourself, "Am I assertive enough to do what I
have to do in order to find my doctor?" This is an important question because so many people seem unable to
act assertively when faced with a physician. I remember
being told by an elderly woman that her husband was
experiencing serious side-effects from the medications
he was taking. "We've told his doctor about it several
times," she said, "but he won't change the prescriptions."
"Have you thought of going to another doctor?" I asked.
"Oh, no, we wouldn't want to do that," she replied, "he's
such a nice man."

Perhaps he is a nice man but for some reason he
was not doing what needed to be done to create trust
and satisfaction in his patient. Nor was his patient

doing what needed to be done to have his concerns addressed. Maybe "we wouldn't want to do that, he's such a nice man" was masking their lack of assertiveness: maybe they were not aware that they, as well as their doctor, had rights and that somehow the rights of all had to be reconciled.

So, now that you are ready to assert yourself to create a good relationship with your doctor you need to define clearly what this good relationship is.

Start by making four lists.

1. The first is a list of your rights or needs in the relationship. What are they? Perhaps: I have a right to a doctor who keeps up with the latest information in his field, I need a doctor who takes time to talk to me, etc. Write your own list.

2. It also means being aware of your doctor's rights or needs. What are they? Write them on your second list.

3. Of course, for us all, rights come with responsibilities. What are your responsibilities as a patient? Perhaps: I have the responsibility to be honest about my medical problems, I have the responsibility to take the medicine he prescribes as directed, etc. Write your third list.

4. What are your doctor's responsibilities? Write your fourth list.

Look at the four lists you have made so far. You probably see that your rights reflect the physician's responsibilities and that his rights reflect your responsibilities. So there is an interlocking area here within which both you and your doctor play your parts. This is an important understanding.

Do you get upset when you believe that you are fulfilling your responsibilities but your physician is not fulfilling his? But is he aware of your expectations? Have you told him? And do you know what constraints he works under as a result of controls by insurance companies and HMOs? These may be preventing him from fulfilling expectations he doesn't even know you have.

So it seems that the best way to find your good doctor is to find out if you and he agree on the criteria you set out. You can do this in three ways: first by asking, then by experiencing and noticing.

Asking

There are some things you can find out only by asking. For example:

- Will he return your phone calls personally or can you speak only to his nurse?
- If you can speak to him on the phone, when is the best time to call?

Make up your own list of what you want to know. You have a right to expect thoughtful answers to your questions but also the responsibility to ask reasonable questions.

Experiencing and Noticing

Other things you find out only by being treated for a medical problem.

- Does he explain what is going on?
- Does he listen to your questions and answer them with good humor?
- Do you like him?
- Would you want to be treated by him if you had a serious illness?
- How did you feel when you left his office?

Make your own list.

If you find that this doctor isn't right for you how do you find others? Obviously, asking friends and acquaintances is a good place to start. If you have a women's center in your city go there and find out if they keep evaluations of doctors based on other women's experiences. Some do. It is here that the issue of seeing a male doctor or a female doctor may come up. Many women today are looking for a woman.

The more people you talk to the more likely you are to find that a few doctors' names are mentioned frequently. If they are not taking any new patients at that time get yourself on a waiting list and then keep calling. You have to find a way to be persistent but not a nuisance, remembering that a doctor with a good reputation is hard to find and worth waiting for.

The disappearance of the old-fashioned family doctor has created a situation where you, the patient, have to go looking in a new way for the doctor who is right for you. But health is a serious matter. Caught between the greedy insurance companies, the controlling HMO's and the overworked doctor, the patient is getting lost. You must always remember that the patient, and the patient's well-being, is what it is all about. We must not let anyone forget that.

THE WINTER TREE
Thoughts on Depression

Surely ours is the only nation that advocates happiness as national policy: "Life, liberty, and the pursuit of happiness." And pursue it we do. We buy things: "when the going gets tough the tough go shopping." And we consume things: food, alcohol, legal drugs, illegal drugs. We spend millions of dollars to mask unhappiness and suffering. Depression is seen as undesirable, an almost shameful condition to be overcome as quickly as possible.

Depression strips us bare. All our assumptions, expectations, pretenses, are torn away. The tearing hurts. We bleed, we cry, we are left helpless, heavy, without hope. The misery seems endless. Never again will we be interested, active, involved. Never again will we feel light, optimistic, energetic.

But depression may be a necessary experience. When we mask it with a drug, when friends attempt to "cheer us up", we are prevented from taking that journey down into the depths of our being. For what is down there? If we allow ourselves to descend might we find precious insights and understanding?

Depression brings the unmentionable right out where it cannot be missed. Life is dark. I am old. I am going to die. I am lonely, afraid, sad, ugly, unwanted. To all of the above say "YES". It is all true. In our youth-obsessed society we are unwanted, we are seen as ugly. For the person who lives alone, life can be lonely. So say a loud "YES" to it all.

Because then something shifts. Out goes the super-ficial promise of the "golden years". Out go the jolly retirement cards, the false reassurances: "I keep busy", "I fill up the time." In comes the reality of being old. It is like a great blessing. It is not fun or happy. It is stark, hard, cold. But it is real and we know it is real. This painful stripping down is a necessary part of life fully lived: not covered up with shopping, TV watching, time-wasting. Depression gives us no place to hide. We come face to face with ourselves. We know who we are.

Consider the winter tree, branches black against the graying sky: authentic, noble, beautiful. The pulse of life is slow as it awaits spring and the unfolding leaves. And so it is for us. For we are part of nature and the natural cycle of darkness and light, winter and spring. Within the great cycle of birth and death we are con-tinually stripped bare, taken down, only to rise again, newly tempered, refined, strengthened, matured.

Yes, I am old and I am going to die. But I look in my mirror and see the special beauty that age has given me. The Pepsi generation may not see it but I do.

Yes, I am old and I am going to die. But I am not unwanted. There are things that only the old can know and can do: things that a long life has given me to offer to the world.

If I am lonely, and sad because I am lonely, then I must change the way I live. To be old does not make me helpless, though the young, with their hard energy, may think that I am. My life is too precious to waste on loneliness. I need the world and the world needs me.

And so we move on, renewed yet again. The dark-ness may return, followed once more by the light. We need them both.

CHOP WOOD, CARRY WATER

Did you chop down a tree this morning? Did you carry water from the well? How long does it take to do the laundry, pulling heavy sheets from the hot, soapy water, their weight sucking them down again, resisting the arms that lug and twist, push and pull? In the days before machines did the work for us our muscles were strong, our bodies firm from the hard labor of living our lives. Today we pay others to provide the energy that does the work. We just push the buttons and our muscles atrophy from lack of use, our bodies accumulate fat.

Do you know that there is a prescription that makes positive changes in the cardiovascular and respiratory system; in muscle strength, bone mass and the flexibility of our joints; in the functioning of our bowels and immune system; in cholesterol levels, sleep patterns, intellectual capacity and depression? Do you know that this wonder-prescription makes you feel better everywhere, that it has an immediate effect on general well-being?

Most people would take this prescription if they could go out and buy it, but it's not something you buy, it's something you do. And that may be why only 8% of the population use this wonder-prescription. What is it?

Aerobic exercise, of course, three times a week for 20 to 30 minutes a time. Every year older people spend hundreds of thousands of dollars on drugs in an effort to maintain well-being but won't spend an hour or two a week on an inexpensive, simple activity (such as walking, bicycling, dancing, swimming) that brings such spectacular improvements in health and general well-being.

It is not that exercise cures the problems many older people experience but that lack of exercise helps to cause and maintain them. Many of the conditions people accept as a normal part of aging are not normal at all. They are the result of inactivity. Many of the conditions that older (or younger) people complain about, consult a doctor about and take medications for, are partly self-induced through lack of exercise.

What is it that a simple exercise like walking does that can promote such an improvement in well-being? Importantly, it is a matter of oxygen. As we age our lungs take in and absorb less oxygen. Our heart pumps less blood per stroke and transports less blood around our body, blood that carries oxygen to the various systems in our body so that they may function. Exercise strengthens our lungs which then absorb more oxygen. Exercise strengthens our heart as well so that it pumps more blood and circulates more oxygen-rich blood around our whole body. Our systems function better. That is why, when we exercise, we feel better all over. That is why exercise improves our total well-being.

When only 8% of the population make the decision to exercise we have to ask ourselves what is going on with the other 92%. I find it hard to believe that they *like* feeling heavy, depressed, sluggish and stiff. I find it hard to believe that they *like* spending unnecessary time and money on doctors' visits and prescriptions.

I find it hard to believe that they *like* feeling sick, grumbling about their problems, worrying about their health, being confined to the house, feeling that strength and joy have gone from their lives.

But maybe I'm wrong. The "sick role", as sociologists call it, is a powerful role. A sick person controls others who live in the same household. The sick person who lives alone gets attention from family, friends and health providers; attention that might otherwise be lacking. Being sick gives a person something to do, something to talk about.

The "sick role" also feeds into the belief that to age is to become sick and useless. "O.K., I'm 65. Now I start to deteriorate," seems to be an underlying assumption of too many people. Old people who are strong and healthy are seen as the exception whereas they should be seen as the norm.

When we were younger many of us abused our bodies with cigarettes, alcohol, food, prescription and over-the-counter drugs. Or we lived in such a way that our bodies suffered from disuse: lack of exercise, lack of mental stimulation, lack of sensory stimulation. Over a lifetime the abuse and disuse eventually catch up with us. Our bodies and minds deteriorate and we presume it is associated with getting older but in fact we are wrong. Such deterioration is not a natural part of getting older. Most of it is associated with not taking reasonable care of our body. This is a shame, because our body is all we have to take us through our life.

There is another reason, I think, why the 92% don't exercise. Our urban-centered lives, our technological times, the machines that do things for us, cut us off from nature and from our own bodies (which are a part of nature). The experience of driving a car for two

miles is of turning the key, shifting the gear, pressing
the pedal, all the time enclosed in a bubble of metal,
glass and plastic. Other than feeling, perhaps, too hot
or too cold (in which case we adjust the temperature),
there is little sense of our body. Its purpose is simply to
make the machine do the work. The body's movements
are simple and undemanding: in fact they become no
more than an extension of the machine.

And the car cuts us off from nature: from the sun
and the wind and the rain: from the sky and the road
going uphill or downhill. In the country the car cuts us
off from the sight of the deer in the woods and the
sound of the seals in the bay.

To walk that two miles is to feel the ground be-
neath your feet, the swing of your arms, the air going
into and out of your lungs, the sun, the wind, the rain
on your face, change in body heat, change in rhythm,
change in blood flow, change in the feeling of being
alive. It is so easy in our technological world to become
cut off from experiencing our body as a sensitive, recep-
tive, responding system, amazingly forgiving, always trying to heal itself, always trying to maintain equilibrium,
always striving to function well and fully. This is no
machine. This is no mere processing plant. This is a
system with a powerful impetus towards physical and
emotional health. When we have been cut off from it
for too long, when it feels sluggish, slow and hurting,
we forget that, while medical care may be needed, there
are things that we can do to help ourselves. Our body
tells us what we need to know but many of us have lost
the ability to listen and to take very seriously what it is
telling us.

There's another problem for the 92% who don't
exercise. When we feel heavy and sluggish it's hard to

find the resolve to exercise. The heaviness and sluggish-ness create a downward spiral. The more sedentary life becomes the more difficult it is to find the will and the physical energy to do the very thing that is needed to reverse the downward spiral. And yet it takes so little to get started. A five-minute walk is enough for the first day, then with small increments of longer time, more energetic walking, we suddenly find that, yes, we're doing it, we feel different, stronger, more vital, better all over. Then our health, endurance and general well-being all improve. Once that has happened we miss it if we stop.

Unfortunately, most doctors, stuck in a narrow medical model, rarely write this wonder-prescription we all need. It is advisable, though, to check with your physician before you get started; then, with approval, go ahead, make your plan and do it.

Here is a reminder that living the gift of age in-volves the participation of all of ourselves. We are not only a body, not only a mind, not only a spiritual self. We are all of these things and they exist within us, not in separate containers, but in a wonderful, demanding, inter-related way. Exercising our body, doing all we can to keep it healthy, improves the way our brain functions. Being in touch with our body links us to nature, reminds us of the part we play in the mystery of being.

And so the mundane, routine demands of living (and exercise may be viewed by some in this way) be-come important, even sacred, as we take seriously our journey through this life.

USING YOUR HEAD
TO SAVE YOUR MIND

L ike a cloud in the sky on a summer's day it hangs there, the dreaded curse of aging. Is he, is she, am I the one who is doomed?

I forgot to buy milk yesterday, I lost my car keys this morning. Is that a sign? The news, the newspapers are full of it. It's the mark of Cain on old people, on some old people... on me?

Alzheimer's disease is its name, after Dr. Alois Alzheimer who identified it in 1906. The reported cases of Alzheimer's disease keep growing. Why is it so much more prevalent? Are we doing something to ourselves? Is it somehow in our food, in our water, in our genes, in the way we live? Can we prevent it? What's going on?

When we read reports on Alzheimer's disease research it seems that we don't know what's going on. We don't know what causes it, we don't know how to cure it, and we don't know for sure who has it. But certainly Alzheimer's exists and certainly it is a most tragic disease, all the more tragic for the uncertainty that surrounds it.

One of the most disturbing aspects of the disease is that it cannot be diagnosed until an autopsy is performed after death and yet I frequently hear people saying with the utmost assurance that a loved one has Alzheimer's. When I inquire about the so-called diagnosis it often seems to have been made on the basis of very little testing. At present even the most sophisticated (and expensive) testing is wrong 25% to 40% of the time. This is a particular tragedy for, when a person is said to have Alzheimer's, no cure is presumed possible so no treatment is attempted. Though the person may be suffering from a treatable condition no cure is sought. Is this simply a case of irresponsible medical care? Is this the sort of thing that could happen to anybody, old or young? Or is there something else going on?

Perhaps we can find an explanation if we look, not at the strictly medical aspects of diagnosis, but at the cultural ones as well. We live in a society where the stereotype of old people is that they are weak, sick and senile. Old people are not valued nor are they respected. The individual old person is often valued, respected and loved by family and friends but the cultural attitude is negative and it is within such a society that an old person lives his life and the elderly population grows. It has more than tripled since 1940. Today there are well over 50 million people over 55. By 2020 that number will have doubled. We are looking at an explosion in the size of a group of people who are vulnerable and, at the same time, are seen to be undesirable.

This negative attitude towards the old is as common among physicians as it is among the general population so it is inevitable that most medical students do not choose to specialize in geriatric medicine. Old people generally suffer from chronic conditions which can never be cured, only monitored; healing is much slower than with younger patients; death is closer to older patients, a difficult fact for many physicians to deal with; and the cultural stereotypes are of a group of people not as attractive or interesting as younger people; smelly, ugly, not nice to touch. This has to affect the way in which some doctors relate to older patients.

So, while there is a desperate need for geriatric physicians the number remains low. In the county where I live, in California, only one physician specializing in geriatric medicine is listed in the yellow pages of the phone book.

The result is that a situation exists where a group of people seen as unwanted and unattractive is growing rapidly while relatively few doctors have the special knowledge or the desire to treat them when they are sick. This is a dangerous situation that can do tragic harm to the unsuspecting elderly and it is the belief of some researchers that it is this situation that affects the diagnosis of Alzheimer's disease; what I call the "wastebasket disease" of old age in America. For if you believe the stereotypes that old people "lose it", then it is too easy to call certain behaviors of memory and behavior, Alzheimer's disease. If you believe that old people are not valuable, then to send them home with the message, "There's nothing we can do," is all part of our cultural assumptions.

The tragedy is that when a person is said to have Alzheimer's disease no cure is possible so no treatment is attempted. The diagnosis becomes, and perhaps unnecessarily, a sentence of slow death. So we need to be very careful, not too trusting. We need to explore, and insist that others explore, alternative explanations for the symptoms of confusion, memory loss and disorientation.

For example, physicians treating an elderly patient too often attribute these symptoms to "senility". They presume the symptoms are part of what they believe to be the normal process of aging. If they were treating a younger person the same symptoms would be explained differently. In fact, confusion and loss of memory are not a normal part of aging and we must never forget this. Most old people score as well as younger people on intelligence tests. Forgetfulness is usually due to slower retrieval of a memory rather than loss of the memory: a very different situation. Further, an illness that is treatable may cause confusion in an old person even though a younger person with the same illness would not experience confusion. The result is that in too many cases the diagnosis is wrong. The patient is not suffering from Alzheimer's. The patient is suffering from a treatable condition.

Another explanation for confusion and loss of memory may be found in the day-to-day habits of the patient. When an old person (or, for that matter, a young person) eats a grossly inappropriate diet, eats so little that he suffers from malnutrition, drinks insufficient fluids, has too little physical exercise, too little sensory stimulation, too little intellectual stimulation and far too many prescription and over-the-counter drugs, symptoms of confusion, loss of memory and erratic behavior can be, and probably will be, the result. If the person is labeled as an Alzheimer's patient nothing is done about the conditions that are responsible for the symptoms. The assumption is that a correct diagnosis has been made.

The problem of over-medication is a serious one for many older patients. Not knowing very much about the older body, many doctors prescribe medication as they would for a younger person. But an older body is not the same as a younger body. For example, because some drugs are metabolized more slowly in the old than in the young they can be dangerous unless carefully prescribed. Sometimes the physician refuses to change the dosage even when the patient complains of the side-effects. There exists an attitude that "doctor knows best" even when he may not know much and the patient knows very well that what is happening is not right.

I have heard tales of old people whose medicine containers fill a grocery bag! I find it almost unbelievable but I have heard it too often to disbelieve it any longer. I was recently present when an 85-year old was found to be taking three medications for water-retention. "And that's two too many," said the nurse who was checking. Medication should be evaluated every so often to prevent over-medication or inappropriate medication. If your doctor is unhelpful, go to your pharmacy and ask the pharmacist to evaluate your overall prescription picture.

The conclusion has to be that Alzheimer's disease may not be quite as much the terrible threat that it is presumed to be. Certainly it exists, and certainly it is most tragic for those who have it and for their loved ones who live with it, but it is possible that a considerable number of those "diagnosed" with the disease are suffering from a treatable condition.

So, yes, there is something we can do. We can pay attention to the details of our life: diet, fluids, exercise, hobbies, activities, seeing friends and family, reaching for emotional wholeness. We can get those medications out of the bathroom cupboard and find out what we are taking, why we are taking it, if the dosage is appropriate, and if there is an undesirable interaction between any of them.

We can also make sure that the presenting symptoms are responsibly evaluated and, if we suspect that they are not, start wondering about our doctor. Does he or she show interest, give undivided attention, welcome questions, have time to get acquainted? Is he warm and compassionate? If not, it is time to change your doctor and go on changing until the right one is found.

We can, and we must, take responsibility for our own well-being and for the well-being of those we love.

The Woman
Guarding the Potatoes
Died of Hunger

Walking into the kitchen, thinking of dinner, I heard her say, "The woman guarding the potatoes died of hunger"; a foreign voice from our little radio describing life as the Soviet Union crumbled in a country with a name I had never heard of, hard to pronounce, impossible to spell.

Not arms, not icons, but potatoes was what she died for. She sacrificed her life for potatoes so that her family, her villagers could live. Sacrifice means giving everything you have, she tells us, sacrifice means death. There is no reward. You give, you give, you get nothing back.

1991 that was, and I think of her again as I grieve over what I see. Not great events, not national upheavals, not a continent crying. No, this time it is families that, afraid of sacrifice, destroy and punish.

I think of the old man, 89, sick, in pain, sitting on the rented, uncurtained commode right there in the living room, his little great-granddaughter leaning against his knee, "What are you doing, grandpa?", his dignity lost. Day after day his wife's voice berating him, criticizing him. His silence, for there is nothing he can say.

I think of the old woman, her life changed in a moment in the doctor's office, the quick, steep race to death a few months away, the family in panic, confusion, handing her over to paid caretakers, wishing it

145

were over, waiting impatiently for her to die so that they can get on with their lives.

I think of the husband tricking his wife into signing away her property then telling her to leave, to live elsewhere. Not with him. He didn't want a sick wife.

I think of the man, only 60, just retired with a good pension, plenty of money, plans to travel with his wife, to reap the reward of years of hard work and family responsibilities. Then cancer, right then, too soon, hospitals and surgery and being sent home to die. No time for even a little cruise. His wife erupted. All the years of unspoken anger blew up. Her fury was terrible, uncontrollable, as he sat, wrapped up by the fire in the California heat, his dreams lost, a future of pain, his wife's accusations accompanying him to the grave.

I have heard things, seen things, that make my blood run cold. Ordinary people, educated people, comfortably-off people, church-going people who, in the face of suffering and death, become unspeakable monsters, do terrible, terrible things to those they love.

I tell myself that they do not mean to be unkind. They have no idea of the misery they create. They cannot comprehend the immensity of their inhumanity. Are they overwhelmed with fear? Does their cruelty come from anger at being cheated of the good times? Are they unable to face suffering and sacrifice? Americans are not accustomed to such experiences. This is the land of opportunity, hope, progress, achievement; of success and the good life. No room here for sickness, for suffering and agony, for death and decay. When these things happen to us we are not prepared for them. When they happen to others we turn away, compassion denied. Those sad, sick people get in the way: no more cruises, mother's comfort lost, the little pile of money threatened. Life is not turning out as promised. No future glows with a comfortable reward.

A sick body in the living room is not in the picture: the intruding paraphernalia of nursing in the bathroom, the unmentionable objects in the waste basket, the unexplained hospital routine. The body that once aroused sexual desire is now hot and dry; the mother, snuggled into for the safety of that enveloping softness and warmth, now clammy and cold, guilty with repulsion.

How can one give up the good life, the real life, for weeks, months, perhaps years of sacrifice? How can one be expected to endure? Care of the sick is for the visiting nurse, the experts, people who know what to do, people who are paid to do it. And how can one go on loving somebody so changed? That is for Mother Teresa. We admire her but cannot emulate her. We're not good enough. We're not saints. We're just ordinary people. We want to enjoy life, not suffer, not sacrifice, for sacrifice means loss, loss of everything, as the woman in that distant land revealed when she sacrificed her life that her friends might live.

For we have forgotten, or maybe never known, that giving is inevitably linked to receiving. To be nurtured is part of nurturing, to be loved is part of loving. The woman who guarded the potatoes did not know this. She did not realize that the potatoes for which she suffered were themselves her nurturers. If she had accepted the nourishment they offered, if she had eaten a few of them, she might have lived.

But even with the understanding that to give is to receive, one is still pulled up short by the enormity of the future. Here are two people, two ordinary people who have lived lives much like everyone else, unexpectedly facing this terrifying, magnificent event. How can they sustain it? How can each contain the vastness of the changes, understandings, feelings, yearnings that will surely happen? How can each acknowledge that, "Yes, here we are. This is it. This is the culmination of our life together. This is where truth lies, and wisdom and understanding and love. Finally we can know each other and ourselves."

We can hide from it, let the professionals take over, or we can recognize the priceless gift, the unforeseen opportunity at last to live our lives together. No time anymore for prevarication, for pretending, for ignoring, for simulating, for denying, for blaming, for wishing things had been different. Time now for surrendering at last to the humanness in each.

In looking after the sick with care and love, tenderly, one comes to accept their situation and, inevitably, one's own. Jesus washed the feet of the poor. What would it mean for the person who did such a thing? For to wash the feet of the poor, to bend, to kneel, to gently hold the dirty, bleeding foot with reverence and respect, changes a person. It changes one's attitude to suffering, sickness and death. In accepting it in another one accepts it in oneself. Life encompasses more. No longer does one deny some part of what it is to be human.

Here is nature's equalizing pattern. Close to the nettle that stings is the plant that heals; near the poison ivy grows the jewel weed balm. If we allow ourselves to express our natural compassion we will not lack nourishment. We do not have to fear. The rewards of a long life lived together will not be lost but they will be changed and the change may be a reward greater than any ever imagined.

For in sharing the suffering of another, in embracing not denying it, in incorporating it willingly into your life, your relationship to the suffering one and to you yourself, changes. You find a depth of closeness undreamed of. The sacrifice of the cruise becomes no sacrifice at all when weighed against the richness of the shared life in that living room, in that hospital room.

Here is time, whatever time is left. Time to review the past, time to be gentle, time to look together at old hurts and, in doing so, feel the cool soft breeze of understanding and forgiveness gently clean the sooty cracks of the past. The long silent hours, holding hands, not against the ship's rail in the romantic sunset, but in the antiseptic, cotton-and-metal hospital room, give nourishment. The relationship changes. There is a depth of closeness undreamed of. The held hand, the shared past, give safety and reassurance to each, for just as the strong hand gives safety to the weak, so the weak gives safety to the strong. When the sick one is dead what will nurture the one who is left? Surely, the sharing of that life of cotton and metal, blood and tears, and the long sweet hours of closeness, of kindness, of talk, of silence.

I recently spoke to a friend whose husband is very ill. For months now she has been tied with him to the house. She spoke of how she has simplified her life, doing less running around, less busy work. She wonders now why she once thought that she must always be on the go. "It seems so unimportant now," she said. "We have peaceful, quiet times together and that's all you need. I'm just grateful for the life we've had. I've found that gratitude is the key to happiness, acceptance the key to serenity." She was telling me that what might have seemed like a sacrifice was no sacrifice, that sharing his sickness and eventual death nourishes her in ways she had never imagined.

Close to the nettle grows the plant that heals.

Moving On

DAISY

We found her living under the house: terrified, starving, dirty, her marmalade-cat coat matted and dull, a cut-off stump for a tail. How had she lost her tail? What torment had she experienced?

We put out a saucer of milk, crouching as we invited her to come, to drink, to join us. But the years had taught her to be careful, to be afraid, to protect herself from harm. Indoors we watched from the window and she came to the milk and drank, hesitantly, ready to scatter to the safety that lay under the house. It took six months before she came into the kitchen. There she would eat and drink but she would not stay. Safety still lay under the house.

Eventually she learned that she was safe with us. She cleaned herself, her marmalade coat became smooth and soft, flesh covered her bones. She sat on our laps and purred. She sat on our friends' laps and purred. For six years she was part of the family. We called her Daisy.

And then she became ill, for she was old. She could not eat, her flesh fell away, her coat again became matted and dull. We talked about her with our gentle veterinarian. We agreed that her life should end.

We were with her as she died, Douglas stroking her head, I her back where the vertebrae felt so touchingly close to my hand. She was purring as the needle went into her paw and then the purring faded away and she was gone, so quietly, so trustingly. Douglas and I cried. We stood in the vet's office, holding each other, and cried over the body of our dead cat.

Now, three days later, I think of how we miss her, our old cat. But what, exactly, are we missing? What was it that she gave to us? What we gave to her is easy to tell. We gave her safety and food and shelter and care and, yes, our love. She received a lot from us. So what did she give in return?

And then I realize that to think about loving in terms of reciprocity is to expect an exchange, to impose an economic, market-place requirement that has nothing to do with the experience. Daisy enriched our lives simply because she was Daisy. That was all and that was enough. To watch her, to hold her, to feel her live, warm essence, stirred within me an atavistic, unfettered, all-accepting, imponderable experience of being. She reminded me, constantly, that out of fear can come trust, that out of misery can come contentment, that to be alive is enough, and that to be alive and touch another living thing is a miracle.

Because she was old and gave so much to us just by being, my thoughts turn to people who are old. So often they see their lives as having little value. They fear becoming a burden on others. Assuming that relationships are based on exchange they believe they have nothing to use as exchange. But a long life has a purpose extraordinary in its value. It is in old age that we finally have the opportunity, even, I would say, the responsibility, to make peace with others and with ourselves; to come to terms with our personal, unique, and often confusing mix of experiences.

Daisy taught me that fear can lead to trust, misery to contentment. We, too, can re-create the disappointments, the failures and the tragedies we have experienced. If we ponder our lives in a spirit of peace and acceptance we find that these hard lessons are strangely bound up with the joys, the successes, even the comedy. It becomes clear that one is necessary for the other. The sadness cannot be separated from the joy, the poverty from the plenty. Each is part of each. We are given it all.

This, then, is the great treasure the old person has for others. This is the inspiration the old may pass down to the young: to accept what one has been given, to accept it all in gratitude, contentment and love. To be alive is enough, to be alive and touch another living thing is a miracle.

Thank you, Daisy.

COMFORT AND HOPE

My friend died last Thursday. Now she no longer exists. Somewhere there is a box, heavy for its size, filled with ash and small pieces of bone. Where, I do not know.

We went to the memorial service. The paintings and the cross were draped with purple cloth, a small choir sang sweetly, the organ roared and fell. I listened to the readings from the New Bible. "Even though I walk in the dark valley I fear no evil; for you are at my side with your rod and your staff that give me courage." I longed for the poetry and passion of the King James edition, "Yea, though I walk through the valley of the shadow of death, I will fear no evil: for thou art with me; thy rod and thy staff they comfort me." The new reading sounded like a writing assignment turned out by a dutiful schoolboy on a bored Friday afternoon.

Click, click, click went my critical mind. I struggled with the difficult story of Job. I heard again Jesus' promise that on his second coming he would lead the dead to his Father in heaven. The priest told us that my friend was already in heaven.

Finally I was able to turn off my clicking mind. The purple drapes took me back to my early years in Italy, to

Rome, Good Friday, the great churches draped in purple, the paintings, the gold, the silver, the heavy, woven tapestries hidden in grief. A time to bow one's body down, down, down, to cover one's face, to feel the pain and the sorrow and the fear, of life, of death, of being human in this world of pain.

Two days later, Easter Sunday. The transformation. The paintings, the gold and silver and tapestry, the flowers, the very building itself, shone and glowed. A time to stretch high, up, up, up to the glory of life, the glory of birth, the glory of rebirth, to start again on this amazing human journey.

I remembered a small, dusty town in Southern Italy. An old peasant woman climbing on her knees up the long, steep, broken steps before the church, her black cloth skirt dragging in the dirt, the toes of her black boots hard and scuffed against the stone, her worn-out hands draped by the delicate fall of her rosary as she did penance for her life of child-bearing, work, poverty, laughter and sorrow. Lord have mercy.

Only then could I be a part of our little memorial service. My intellectual questions were beside the point. We were there for the ritual that could give us comfort and could give us hope: the ritual of coming together, of entering, of signing the book, of being with each other, of remembering, weeping, hearing the words, the memories, the songs, of listening to the story that promised redemption, transcendence, salvation. Comfort and hope. That is what we were there for. The old peasant woman, knees against the hard stone, bones hurting with age and work, prayed for forgiveness and comfort and hope.

All cultures offer reassurance in their own way. All religions have their story of inspiration but the story does not matter. One believes it or does not believe it. It is the act of coming together that acknowledges the friend that is no more, that tells us, each one of us sitting there, that one day we will be no more, that we, too, will be in a box, heavy for its size, of ashes and a few small pieces of bone. We have to go down, we have to drag our skirts in the dust, and as we go down we have to hope, we have to hope that in this life, or perhaps another, we may know redemption, transcendence, salvation.

Lying in bed that night, finally understanding, the tears pricked and fell. I could only reach in the dark for my love and gently stroke his sleeping face with my hand. Lord have mercy upon us.

BUDDHA SMILES

e found the Buddha in the bushes. As the
years had passed the garden had grown
around him, the house fallen into disrepair,
the old couple died. We were among those that went to
the estate sale just looking for a bargain, unaware of the
history, of the lives that had been lived there. We
brought our Buddha home and put him in our garden,
out in the rain, the sun, the wind. Birds sit on his head.
He broods. He smiles.

I suppose we paid for our Buddha with a check,
with our address, for we are occasionally notified of other
sales. So it was that I found out that my dead friend's
estate was being sold and we went to another estate
sale. This time I knew the house, the history. I knew the
life she had lived there. I was looking for a little piece of
her that I could take home with me, a little piece of her
reality that would become mine.

I entered the house with the others. They did not
know her. They were just looking for a bargain. "Lots of
good stuff," a departing man told us as we entered. And
there I was, seeing it all again. But now strangers were
rummaging through her clothes in the closet, checking
out her large library. I looked at the bed where she had
lain. No one had bought that yet. The chair I used to
pull up, close, so I could hold her hand, had gone, to

another house I suppose. Other people who did not know her would sit on it, then gradually it would become "theirs", part of their lives.

I cried. I stood in the kitchen, wondering about wooden spoons, and I cried. I cried that she died too young. I cried for both the evil and the love that had surrounded her. I cried that her private life was now invaded by all these well-meaning strangers. I cried that things had to come to an end. I left the house with my little collection of memorabilia.

Now, today, I realize that I had got used to her being dead but I had not reckoned with the disbursement of her belongings. As long as they remained in that house it was as if she remained there as well. The book, with her notations in the margin, on the shelf where she had placed it, carried the energy of her reading, her writing, her scholarship, her selection of where to place it on the shelf. But now that the book was gone, thrown onto the back seat of a stranger's car, put on a different shelf in a different room, where was she? Does every change of book, of wooden spoon, of chair, remove her, little by little, from the world?

It felt like that, as I stood in that house invaded by strangers. But now I realize that I was wrong. I am being forced to pay attention to the cosmos and it is telling me that nothing has changed. I, my dead friend, everybody and everything in this world and in this universe are in a continual state of flux, of disintegration that leads to regeneration, of decay that leads to renewal, of crisis that leads to opportunity, of the planet Earth turning, turning, as the sun rises and sets, only to rise and set, rise and set once more, once more, once more.

The chair I sat in as I held her hand and talked of death has gone from my physical world. Now it is part of another's physical world. But the memory of those hours will never leave me. I have to remember that the chair was not the solid matter it appeared to be. And, even more importantly, I have to remember that my memory of all that passed between us in that room has an existence as real, more real, than that of the chair. The experience changed me and so must change others. Some part of my children, my beloved, my friends, all unaware, will be affected by my experience as we are all affected by everything in this interrelated, interconnected system of which each one of us is a part. The chair-experience cannot go away. Others may kick the material chair, paint it red, throw it on the bonfire, but my chair-experience cannot go away. It cannot help but be passed on, then passed on, then, again, passed on. It does not matter that her "things" are gone to other homes. It is her essence, her energy, her living at all that is the stuff of eternity.

The Buddha sits and smiles. It was he who started all this. Without him I would not have known about the sale, would not have had the experience in the house, would not have cried, would not have understood, would not have written this essay which you are reading, would not have affected, in some way, you. We cannot help but live on in this cohesive, interrelated world. Perhaps that is why Buddha smiles.

MORE BOOKS TO READ

Here is a list of a few of the books on my shelves. They constitute just a glimpse into the world of aging and matters associated with this challenging and exciting time in our lives.

One of the delights of reading is the way that one book inevitably leads to another, especially when a book includes quotations from other writers that whet one's appetite for more, or when there's a reading list at the end. Then the chase is on, a chase that can lead anywhere: to deeper knowledge in one area or moving out into related areas of interest in a never-ending web of knowledge, inquiry and satisfaction.

I find that I have become a compulsive library-user. I can't imagine how I'd get along without my public library. It's free, it's efficient, it's stuffed with books that I just have to read, and the staff are astonishingly helpful and patient.

They never seem to tire of getting me books from other branches then calling me to let me know that yet more exciting treasures are there, just waiting for me to pick them up.

For those who are unable to get to the library or who live in a rural area where there is no library, the book-mobile is an important link with this world of books. The van carries its own collection, but reference services and interlibrary loan services are available if you can't find what you want.

The library is an excellent place to find a book to read without the expense of buying it, to browse along a shelf in search of related books with the same Dewey number, and to find books that are out of print so can't be bought. If you have access to a public library or to a college/university library you have the whole world in your hands in a book.

Marsha Sinetar has written several books that can be helpful and inspirational to those of us who are aging even though she does not write specifically for older people.

> • Ordinary People as Monks and Mystics by Marsha Sinetar, published by Paulist Press, 1986. Sinetar writes, at the beginning of this book, "It has been said that whoever finds out what is, for him, good, and holds fast to it, will become whole." This book is based on the stories of ordinary people who sought to do that.

> • Do What You Love, the Money Will Follow by Marsha Sinetar, published by Dell Publishing, 1987. This book is about people who do the work they enjoy, sometimes leaving a well-paid job they hate, trusting that "the money will follow." If you have retirement income that takes care of basic needs this is the perfect time to "do what you love."

Books on solitude are helpful because they tell us that others share our disappointing ambivalence and frustration with being alone for long periods of time as well as our joy when we experience the inner peace that solitude can bring. You might want to look at:

- Fifty Days of Solitude by Doris Grumbach, published by Beacon Press, 1994.

- Solitude: A Return to the Self by Anthony Storr, published by Ballantine Books, 1988.

There exists an interesting and growing collection of books on new approaches to illness and health. While acknowledging that Western medicine does wonderful things, many people (and a growing number of physicians) are finding that healing is helped by other methods: relaxation, prayer, the Therapeutic Touch, visualization, meditation, the spiritual development of forgiveness and wholeness, and so on. New understanding of the mind/body relationship does not in any way denigrate the important part played by Western medical knowledge but shows that both Western treatment and alternative healing methods are necessary.

- Love, Medicine and Miracles by Bernie Siegal, M.D. published by Harper & Row, 1986. Siegal writes about what he calls "exceptional patients", or survivors. Refusing to participate in defeat, they show that the mind can dramatically affect the body.

- Peace, Love and Healing by the same author, 1989.

- <u>Getting Well Again</u> by O. Carl Simonton and S. Matthews-Simonton, published by Bantam Books, 1978. This is one of the classics on using mind-body techniques in the treatment of cancer.

- <u>Anatomy of an Illness</u> by Norman Cousins, published by Bantam Books, 1981. The now famous story of Cousins' use of laughter to fight a dangerous disease.

- <u>The Uncommon Touch: an Investigation of Spiritual Healing</u> by Tom Harpur, published by McClelland & Stewart Inc., 1994. In this beautifully written book, Tom Harpur, a Canadian writer on religion and ethics, examines evidence on a wide range of non-medical healing.

- <u>Spontaneous Healing</u> by Andrew Weil, M.D. published by Ballantine Books, 1995. Each one of us is born with a natural healing system, says Weil. By paying attention to our daily health we can tap into the sources of health within.

Now a couple of books on growing old, very different from each other, but each with something to add to our experience of ourselves:

- <u>Winter Grace: Spirituality for the Later Years</u> by Kathleen Fischer, published by Paulist Press, 1985. Fischer, who teaches theology at Seattle University, shows how Christian spirituality transforms aging into winter grace.

• <u>The Art of Growing Older,</u> edited by Wayne Booth, published by Poseidon Press, 1992. A collection of poems and thoughts on aging written by many well-known writers then woven into an engaging aggregate by the editor.

Retirement raises the question of how to live a fulfilling life now that paid work outside the home has ended. Some realize that it is through service to others that self-fulfillment becomes possible.

In my opinion, by far the best book on service is:

• <u>Compassion in Action: Setting Out on the Path of Service</u> by Ram Dass and Mirabai Bush, published by Bell Tower, 1992. The book's powerful message to the reader may be summed up in a quotation from the Dalai Lama, "Love and compassion are necessities, not luxuries. Without them, humanity cannot survive." There is an excellent bibliography which includes books to read and organizations to get in touch with that are "working for positive change in the world".